FOR BOSTON

We didn't just
win it.
We won it
AT HOME.

LARRY LUCCHINO

The Boston Globe

This book is available in quantity at special discounts for your group or organization.
For further information, contact:

Triumph Books LLC
814 North Franklin Street
Chicago, Illinois 60610
Phone: (312) 337-0747
www.triumphbooks.com

Printed in U.S.A.
ISBN: 978-1-60078-892-5

TRIUMPH
BOOKS

BOOK STAFF

EDITOR Janice Page
ASSISTANT EDITOR/WRITER Ron Driscoll
ART DIRECTOR Rena Anderson Sokolow
DESIGNER Cindy Daniels
PROOFREADERS Paul Colton, William Herzog, Richard Kassirer, Kevin Coughlin

PHOTOGRAPHERS

THE BOSTON GLOBE Yoon S. Byun, 87 • Barry Chin, front cover, 13, 19-20, 26, 28, 46-48, 54, 71, 78, 87, 93-94, 100 • Jim Davis, 7, 11-12, 14, 16, 18, 20, 24, 27, 29, 32-37, 43-45, 48-50, 54, 56-68, 77, 81, 89, 94, 105, 113, 125, 127 • Stan Grossfeld, 15, 17, 23, 30, 40-41, 128 • Matthew J. Lee, 72-75, 82, 107, 109 • Jessica Rinaldi, 86-87 • John Tlumacki, 2, 54, 68, 95 • file photos, 121-122.

ADDITIONAL PHOTOS COURTESY OF
AP/WIDE WORLD PHOTOS 1, 8, 126 (David J. Phillip) • 5, 52, 116 (Charlie Riedel) • 41, 51, 124 (Matt Slocum) • 84, 87 (Michael Dwyer) • 96 (Mark J. Terrill) • back cover (Charles Krupa). ELSA/GETTY IMAGES 6 (Rob Carr) • 22 (Ronald Martinez) • 38, 92, 99, 111 (Jared Wickerham) • 90 (Jim Rogash) • 97-98 (Al Messerschmidt) • 124 (Al Bello).

With special thanks to Boston Globe publisher Christopher Mayer and editor Brian McGrory; Joe Sullivan, Tim Healey, Luke Knox, and the Boston Globe sports department; Bill Greene, Jim Wilson, and the Globe photo department; Lisa Tuite, Jeremiah Manion, and the Globe library staff; Globe executive director of communications Ellen Clegg; Mary Zanor, John Gates, and Elevate Communications; Mitch Rogatz, Kristine Anstrats, and everyone at Triumph Books; Jim Karaian, Jay Layman, Chris Jackson and Quad/Graphics of Taunton; Todd Shuster, Lane Zachary, and Zachary Shuster Harmsworth Literary Agency.

Front cover Koji Uehara and Jarrod Saltalamacchia celebrate clinching the ALCS over the Detroit Tigers.

Back cover A rainbow presages the opening of the World Series at Fenway Park.

CONTENTS

Fans on Yawkey Way celebrate Boston's first world title since 2007.

The World Series Trophy made the rounds, from team owners Larry Lucchino, Tom Werner, and John Henry (right) to the players who brought it home to Fenway Park.

INTRODUCTION

BY LARRY LUCCHINO

Through many seasons, successful or not, there has been a durable bond between the people of Boston and New England and their baseball team. This season, the simple act of coming together on a spring night in Fenway Park took on a different meaning.

After the April 15 Marathon bombings shattered lives and shook our city deeply, Bostonians and New Englanders responded with love, quiet compassion, and tremendous resolve. Starting on April 20, with the first home stand after the bombing, the Red Sox determined to recognize the tragedy, pay tribute to victims and first responders all season long, while still providing common ground and the diversion of a summer game.

Playing games during a time of crisis may seem to some in questionable taste. But to move forward seemed a solemn obligation. New Englanders proved resilient, showing that while adversity may temporarily set us back, we would not allow any hardship, any calamity, any misfortune to keep us down for long. The team was no different: "This is our (bleeping) city."

All through the summer, our ballpark was like a neighbor's porch where all were welcome to come and sit and share in the fortunes of a team. They came for distraction and comfort. They came for the solace of simply gathering together. More and more, the team took on the character of the city, borrowing from its ample store of resilience and determination.

The Red Sox played with grit and resolve. Time and again, this team came from behind to win in all sorts of unexpected and miraculous ways. Our club began to rise from the great disappointment of September 2011 and the last-place finish of 2012. Tapping into the innate optimism and inner strength of people familiar with hard times, the city and New England moved forward through the smoke of April into the clear October light.

At our introductory press conference in December 2001, John Henry, Tom Werner, and our ownership group made five commitments to New England and all of Red Sox Nation. The first of these obligations was to "field a team worthy of the fans' support." This took on an entirely new meaning for us in 2013.

To be certain, baseball matters. Not always so much the winning and losing. President Franklin Delano Roosevelt recognized this when, after Pearl Harbor, he urged then-commissioner Kenesaw Mountain Landis to continue playing the games while the country was at war. Boston is a city of many races, ethnicities, traditions, and faiths; no single one embraces us all. Then there is baseball; the Red Sox bring this city and region together as one large congregation of fans. In times of trial and difficulty, baseball provides us a reason to gather and draw strength from our community. And so it was this season, this World Championship season, 2013.

Larry Lucchino is president and CEO of the Boston Red Sox.

SERIES

IN A MATCHUP OF 97-GAME WINNERS, THE RED SOX CONSISTENTLY PRODUCED THE BIG PITCH AND THE BIG HIT.

REWARD

The Red Sox storm the field after winning their eighth world title.

8-1	STL	0 0 0	0 0 0	0 0 1	1 7 3
	BOS	3 2 0	0 0 0	2 1 x	8 8 1

GAME 1 WEDNESDAY 10/23/2013 • FENWAY PARK OOOOOOO

4-2	STL	0 0 0	1 0 0	3 0 0	4 7 1
	BOS	0 0 0	0 0 2	0 0 0	2 4 2

GAME 2 THURSDAY 10/24/2013 • FENWAY PARK OOOOOOO

VS ST. LOUIS

5-4	BOS	0 0 0	0 1 1	0 2 0	4 6 2
	STL	2 0 0	0 0 0	2 0 1	5 12 0

GAME 3 SATURDAY 10/26/2013 • BUSCH STADIUM OOOOOOO

4-2	BOS	0 0 0	0 1 3	0 0 0	4 6 2
	STL	0 0 1	0 0 0	1 0 0	2 6 0

GAME 4 SUNDAY 10/27/2013 • BUSCH STADIUM OOOOOOO

3-1	BOS	1 0 0	0 0 0	2 0 0	3 9 0
	STL	0 0 0	1 0 0	0 0 0	1 4 0

GAME 5 MONDAY 10/28/2013 • BUSCH STADIUM OOOOOOO

6-1	STL	0 0 0	0 0 0	1 0 0	1 9 1
	BOS	0 0 3	3 0 0	0 0 x	6 8 1

GAME 6 WEDNESDAY 10/30/2013 • FENWAY PARK OOOOOOO

IT

BY DAN SHAUGHNESSY • Globe Staff

BACK BAY a party unlike anything since 1918. » Six months after Shelter in Place, the city of Boston invites the world to celebrate a victory of team over self. Boston Strong, at least a variation of the theme, hit a crescendo on October on the Fenway lawn, the town common of 2013. The 2013 Red Sox, the motley crew that left Fort Myers begging, "Please don't hate us," completed the ultimate redemption song, thrashing the St. Louis Cardinals, 6-1, in the sixth and final game of the World Series. The Brotherhood of the Beard are World Champions for the third time this century, worthy progeny of the 20th century Sox, who won five of the first 15 Series back in the days when Babe Ruth was a fuzzy-faced lefthanded orphan from Baltimore. » Nobody saw this coming. Nobody. After the worst season in 47 years — the Bobby Valentine clown show of 2012 — Sox general manager Ben Cherington and new field manager John Farrell made the Red Sox relevant and good again. The 2013 Sox dusted the field in the American League East, then blew past the Tampa Bays Rays, the Detroit Tigers, and the estimable Cardinals in an 11-5 postseason onslaught. The Sox were dominant. In the 2013 playoffs they bested aces Matt Moore, David Price, Justin Verlander, Max Scherzer, Anibal Sanchez, Adam Wainwright, and Michael Wacha. » And so Boston has its eighth championship parade since 2002, and outgoing mayor Thomas Menino will be on a duck boat, which is scheduled to roll down Boylston Street, past the places where the bombs exploded on Marathon Monday, April 15. It is the ultimate civic comeback story. » These are the 2013 Red Sox. They finished in the basement of the American League East in 2012, winning a mere 69 games in a trainwreck season that came on the heels of the epic collapse of the Terry Francona/Theo Epstein Sox who folded dramatically in September 2011. > PAGE 21

For Jonny Gomes, whose home run won Game 4, it was time to don the helmet and wave the banner.

St. Louis shortstop Pete Kozma drops the relay throw as Boston's Dustin Pedroia (15) barrels into second base in the first inning. Umpire Dana DeMuth initially called Pedroia out, leading Boston manager John Farrell (below, top) to argue the blown call. All six umpires huddled, then reversed DeMuth and called Pedroia safe, leading St. Louis manager Mike Matheny (22) to argue his case with crew chief John Hirschbeck. The Red Sox took a 3-0 lead in the inning. advanced to the ALCS.

what
was
that?

8-1

W S [1]

LESTER VS WAINWRIGHT

David Ortiz soars into home on a three-run double by Mike Napoli as the Red Sox quickly take control of Game 1. An inning later, Ortiz's bid for a grand slam was thwarted by Carlos Beltran (below), but the Sox made it 5-0 on the play and Beltran left the game an inning later with a rib injury after slamming into the wall on his catch.

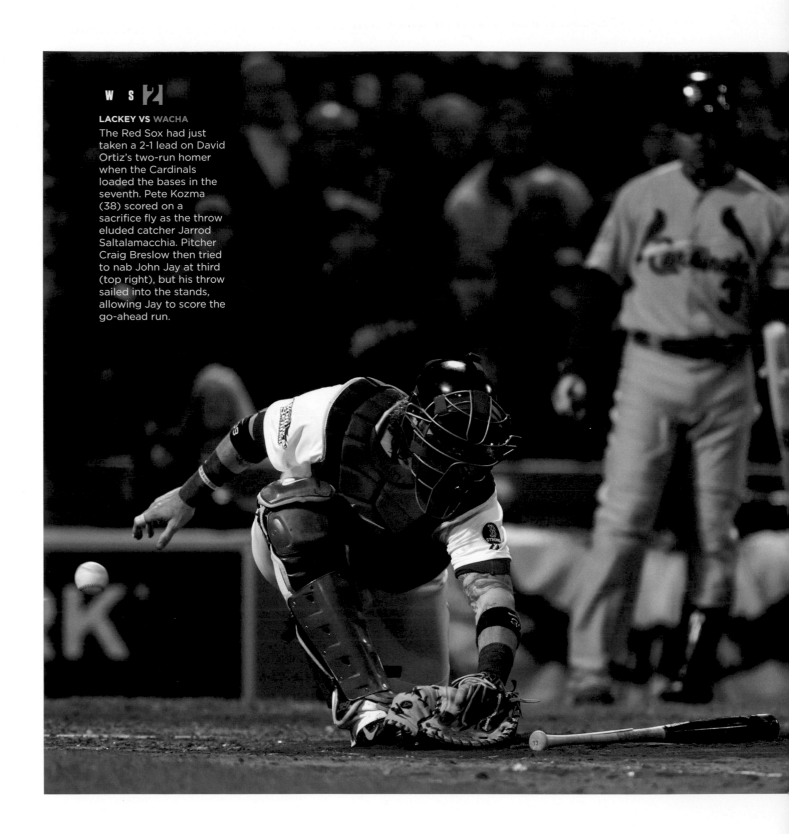

W S 12

LACKEY VS WACHA

The Red Sox had just taken a 2-1 lead on David Ortiz's two-run homer when the Cardinals loaded the bases in the seventh. Pete Kozma (38) scored on a sacrifice fly as the throw eluded catcher Jarrod Saltalamacchia. Pitcher Craig Breslow then tried to nab John Jay at third (top right), but his throw sailed into the stands, allowing Jay to score the go-ahead run.

4-2

what was that?

5-4

W S 3

PEAVY VS KELLY

The game-ending sequence included Dustin Pedroia diving to snare a grounder and throwing out Yadier Molina (4) at home; Jarrod Saltalamacchia throwing wide of third base as Allen Craig tried to advance; Craig heading for home but being thrown out by left fielder Daniel Nava; and home-plate umpire Dana DeMuth calling Craig safe, pointing to an obstruction call by third-base umpire Jim Joyce on Will Middlebrooks, who got tangled with Craig as he attempted to score.

4-2

W S 4

BUCHHOLZ VS LYNN

Jonny Gomes, a late addition to the lineup, belts a three-run homer to give Boston a 4-1 lead in the sixth inning, after starter Clay Buchholz (right) had overcome shoulder fatigue to give the Sox four innings of work, allowing one unearned run. Felix Doubront and John Lackey helped get the game to the ninth inning (Page 23), with Lackey pitching a scoreless eighth in his first relief appearance in nine years.

THE SOX
join the 1991 Minnesota Twins as the only teams to win a World Series one season after finishing in last place.

LACKEY
becomes the first starting pitcher to earn Series-clinching wins with two teams: the Red Sox and the 2002 Angels.

UEHARA
recorded 7 saves, matching the record for one postseason. Four others have done it, with the Phillies' Brad Lidge (2008) the most recent.

ORTIZ
is now the first non-Yankee to win three world titles with one team since Jim Palmer with the Orioles (1966, 1970, and 1983).

BOSTON
is 8-4 in 12 World Series trips. Their eight world titles are fourth all-time, behind the Yankees (27), Cardinals (11), and Athletics (9).

FROM 10 • John Lackey was the poster boy of the 2011 chicken-and-beer chokers, and in Game 6 this year he completed his comeback ballad, hurling 6 innings of one-run ball and becoming the first man in baseball history to start and win World Series-clinching games for two franchises (Lackey won Game 7 for the Angels over the Giants when he was a 24-year-old rookie in 2002). The Boston pariah of 2011 became the hero of 2013.

This finale was the first World Series Game 6 at Fenway since the Carlton Fisk Home Run Game of 1975, and it was a worthy successor. Luis Tiant, the '75 Game 6 starter, and his old batterymate Fisk threw out ceremonial first pitches, and Sox heartbeat Dustin Pedroia completed the metaphor when he hit a towering foul fly that narrowly missed the left-field pole in the bottom of the first.

Pedroia's near-miss was a mere footnote. The Sox would not be denied.

Both teams squandered scoring opportunities in the first two innings. It looked like it might be a true contest, but the Sox removed all doubt with a three-run third off St. Louis rocket boy Wacha.

Jacoby Ellsbury led with a single to right. After Pedroia went out on a grounder to third, Wacha

intentionally walked World Series MVP David Ortiz (.688). Good move. Mike Napoli struck out and then Jonny Gomes was hit by a pitch to load the bases.

Enter Shane Victorino. Cue the music. "Three Little Birds," by Bob Marley.

Every little thing gonna be all right.

Victorino turned on a 2-1 pitch and drove it toward the Monster Seats. The ball hit the Covidien sign on the wall, good for three runs and a World Series ring. Victorino was credited with a three-run double. The ballgame was over.

The Sox added three more runs and chased Wacha in the fourth. Much-maligned Stephen Drew led off with a homer into the Red Sox bullpen (gloved by Franklin Morales), and surrendered a double to Ellsbury. The young righthander (MVP of the NLCS) was lifted after intentionally walking Ortiz. Napoli made it 5-0 with a single to center off Lance Lynn. After a walk to Gomes, Victorino struck again with a single to left and it was 6-0. Ballgame.

There was good drama for the Sox in the seventh. With two out and nobody aboard, the Cardinals rallied with a single, a double, and Carlos Beltran's RBI single. Farrell came out to get Lackey, but was rebuffed.

"This is my game!" Lackey shouted to his manager.

Farrell relented. But when Lackey walked Matt Holliday to load the bases, the manager reemerged from the dugout and pulled his starter. When Lackey walked off the mound, he tipped his cap to the masses who'd rightfully crushed him over the past two years. Junichi Tazawa retired Allen Craig on a harmless grounder and it was on to the seventh-inning stretch.

It was a mere formality in the last two innings. Indomitable Sox closer Koji Uehara came out for the ninth and retired the side in order, sealing the championship by striking out Matt Carpenter (swinging) at 11:23 p.m.

Fifteen minutes after the final out, Red Sox/Globe owner John Henry hoisted the World Series championship trophy ("The World Series Cup," according to Menino) and addressed the crowd as fireworks smoke enveloped the infield. Henry spoke. Tom Werner spoke. Cherington spoke. And then Farrell took center stage for his bow.

It was the first time the Sox won the World Series on the Fenway lawn since Carl Mays beat the Chicago Cubs in Game 6 on Sept. 11, 1918.

Ninety-five years later, the Sox won it again on their home field. And the party lingered long into the night.

what was that?

Boston closer Koji Uehara points to first baseman Mike Napoli after they combined to pick off St. Louis pinch runner Kolten Wong for the final out of Game 4. With Carlos Beltran representing the tying run at the plate, Uehara caught Wong leaning the wrong way to end a World Series game on a pickoff for the first time. "I just got a little off the base," said Wong. "Wanted to go back, and my foot slipped on me. ... I just got too far off and he made a good throw."

'That was wild. That was awesome. It was kind of like last night. I bet they're dumbfounded, like, "What just happened?"'

DAVID ROSS

3-1

LESTER VS WAINWRIGHT

David Ross pats Jon Lester on the shoulder just before Lester was removed from the game after 7⅔ innings. Lester allowed four hits, including a solo homer to Matt Holliday — the first run he has allowed in three World Series career starts – to stake the Red Sox to a 3-2 Series lead. David Ortiz gave Boston a 1-0 lead with an RBI double in the first inning, and Ross had the go-ahead RBI double in the seventh.

6-1

WS 6

LACKEY VS WACHA

Jacoby Ellsbury and Xander Bogaerts — and more importantly, home-plate umpire Jim Joyce — signal Jonny Gomes safe on Shane Victorino's bases-clearing double in the third inning. For Victorino (18) — who had been 0 for 10 in the World Series before the wall-ball double, and missed Games 4 and 5 with a back injury — the hit echoed his grand slam that won Game 6 of the ALCS for Boston, when he stepped in at 2 for 23 in the series.

Red Sox manager John Farrell joins John Lackey and Red Sox infielders in a seventh-inning mound conference, during which Lackey persuaded Farrell to leave him in to pitch to the Cardinals' Matt Holliday. When Lackey walked Holliday, his night was over. Stephen Drew (right) — just 1 for 16 in the Series to that point — was well received after his fourth-inning solo homer. It wasn't a save situation, but Koji Uehara (next page) celebrated after closing out the team's fourth clinching victory of 2013 (AL East pennant, ALDS, ALCS).

PENNANT

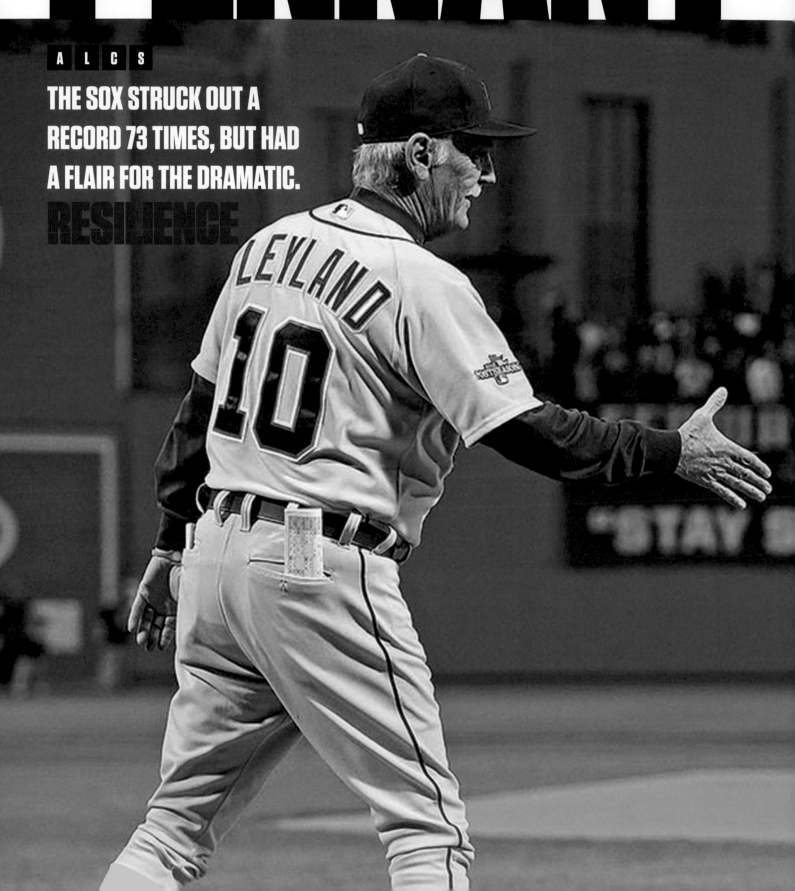

THE SOX STRUCK OUT A RECORD 73 TIMES, BUT HAD A FLAIR FOR THE DRAMATIC.

RESILIENCE

1-0	DET	0 0 0	0 0 1	0 0 0	1 9 0
	BOS	0 0 0	0 0 0	0 0 0	0 1 1

GAME 1 SATURDAY 10/12/2013 • FENWAY PARK ○○○○○○○

6-5	DET	0 1 0	0 0 4	0 0 0	5 8 1
	BOS	0 0 0	0 0 1	0 4 1	6 7 1

GAME 2 SUNDAY 10/13/2013 • FENWAY PARK ○○○○○○○

1-0	BOS	0 0 0	0 0 0	1 0 0	1 4 0
	DET	0 0 0	0 0 0	0 0 0	0 6 1

GAME 3 TUESDAY 10/15/2013 • COMERICA PARK ○○○○○○○

7-3	BOS	0 0 0	0 0 1	1 0 1	3 12 0
	DET	0 5 0	2 0 0	0 0 x	7 9 0

GAME 4 WEDNESDAY 10/16/2013 • COMERICA PARK ○○○○○○○

4-3	BOS	0 3 1	0 0 0	0 0 0	4 10 0
	DET	0 0 0	0 1 1	1 0 0	3 10 1

GAME 5 THURSDAY 10/17/2013 • COMERICA PARK ○○○○○○○

5-2	DET	0 0 0	0 0 2	0 0 0	2 8 1
	BOS	0 0 0	0 1 0	4 0 x	5 5 1

GAME 6 SATURDAY 10/19/2013 • FENWAY PARK ○○○○○○○

VS DETROIT

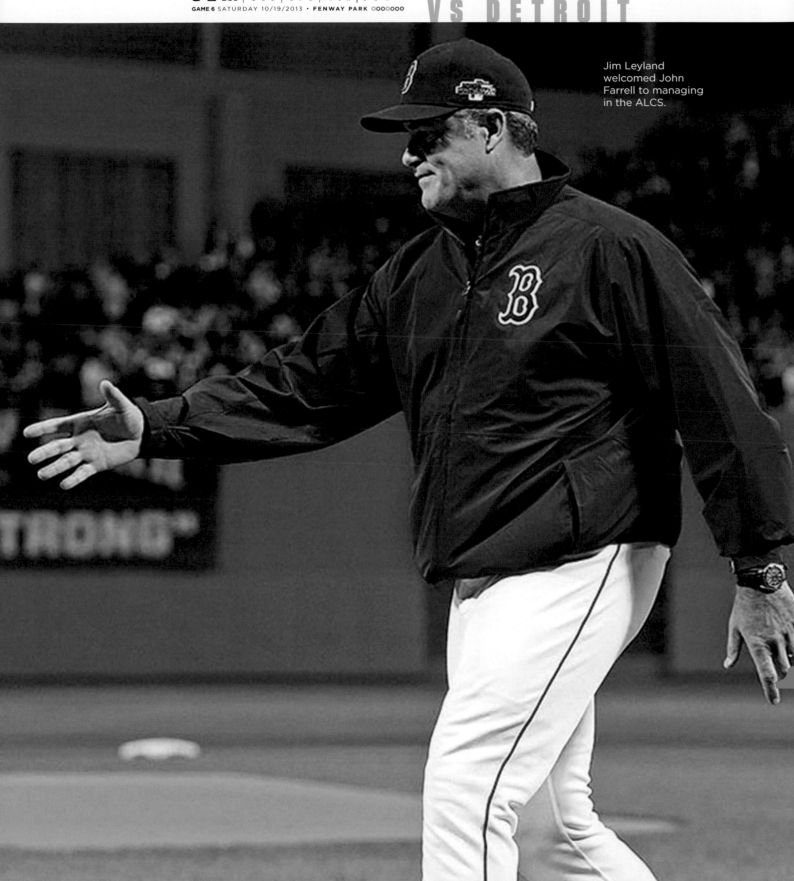

Jim Leyland welcomed John Farrell to managing in the ALCS.

IT

BY DAN SHAUGHNESSY • Globe Staff

...WAS JUST BE... ...on a splendid Saturday night at our 101-year-old ballpark wh... ...m Hawaii stepped to the plate as we heard the recording of a m... ...Jamaica singing, "Don't worry about a thing, 'cause every little thing... ...right." » More than 38,000 voices sang along with Bob Marley... Shane Victorino effectively ended eight days and six games of unforgettable baseball with a grand slam into the Monster Seats on an 0-2 pitch from Tigers reliever Jose Veras. » The Flyin' Hawaiian's shot bookended the bases-loaded blast by Dave Ortiz that kickstarted everything one week ago, and launched the Red Sox into the 2013 World Series. » Boston's American League Championship Series clincher, a 5-2 Sox victory, officially ended at 12:01 Sunday morning when Koji Uehara fanned Jose Iglesias, triggering a wild celebration on the Fenway infield and pandemonium in the stands and streets outside the park. One year after enduring last-place humiliation and the worst season in 47 years, the Red Sox were AL champions for the 13th time since 1901. » It all started one year ago, when general manager Ben Cherington hired Blue Jays manager John Farrell. He was the perfect candidate to replace clown prince Bobby Valentine. He was a pitching coach with the 2007 world champion Red Sox and already had the respect of veterans Dustin Pedroia, David Ortiz, Jacoby Ellsbury, Jon Lester, Clay Buchholz, and John Lackey. » Cherington did the rest. In the winter of 2012-13, he went after quality clubhouse veterans, players who had played in big markets and big games. He acquired Jonny Gomes, Mike Napoli, David Ross, Ryan Dempster, Uehara, and Victorino. » And they all contributed mightily. They changed the clubhouse culture. » "I felt it the first day of spring training," Pedroia said in midseason when the Sox were fending off injuries and challenges. "We were all about › PAGE 41

After Koji Uehara gave the Red Sox a lift with a five-out save in Game 5, David Ortiz returned the favor.

1-0

ALCS 1

LESTER VS SANCHEZ

With the tying run on second base, Xander Bogaerts reacts to hitting a popup to end Game 1. The Red Sox managed just one hit— a Daniel Nava single in the ninth — and struck out 17 times against Anibal Sanchez and four Tiger relievers, and Jhonny Peralta's RBI single in the sixth was all that Detroit needed.

ALCS

BUCHHOLZ VS SCHERZER

David Ortiz sends the game-tying grand slam on its way (previous page), barely out of the reach of Tigers' right fielder Torii Hunter as Boston policeman Steve Horgan celebrates. Detroit closer Joaquin Benoit (right) knows that he has awakened the Red Sox offense, after it had managed no runs and one hit in the first 14 innings of the series.

FROM 34 • winning, right from the start."

And they won. They won 97 games. They demolished the Rays in a four-game Division Series.

Then came the mighty Tigers, champions of the Central Division, a team with a 68-year-old universally respected manager, a stable of big, slow sluggers, and the best starting rotation in baseball.

The Sox beat the Tigers in six pulsating games. It was a series with dozens of freeze-frame moments, none more memorable than Ortiz's iconic blast into the Red Sox bullpen that brought the Sox back from a 5-1 deficit in the critical second game. The photo of inverted Torii Hunter and the celebrating Boston cop will be the signature moment of this series, maybe of the entire season. Uehara was named series MVP, but it just as well could have been Big Papi, even though he only managed two hits in the six games.

Buchholz needed 17 minutes to pitch to four batters to get through the top of the first. As great as these games were, the pace (3:52 in Game 6) was not baseball's friend. Grinding out at-bats is one thing; hideous delay is quite another. The pace of these games is a serious threat to the erstwhile National Pastime.

We almost had a reenactment of Carlton Fisk's 1975 midnight moonshot off the foul pole in the third when Pedroia annihilated a first pitch from Max Scherzer, driving it deep into the night, mere inches left of the pole. Pedroia didn't have quite enough body English as he moved down the first-base line and the ball sailed foul. Instead of a three-run homer, Pedroia wound up grounding into a double play to keep things scoreless.

Thanks to wonderboy Xander Bogaerts, the Sox broke through with a run in the fifth. The X-Man, Boston's youngest postseason starter since Babe Ruth, set things up with a two-out double off the Wall in left center (near the "B Strong" emblem). He came around to score when Jacoby Ellsbury cracked the next pitch into right field. The pitch Bogaerts hit was a 100-mile-per-hour fastball.

The Tigers answered with two in the sixth, but should have had more. Farrell lifted Buchholz (85 pitches) after a walk and Miguel Cabrera's single started the inning. Franklin Morales was Farrell's reliever of choice and it was a disaster. The lefty walked useless Prince Fielder on four pitches, then surrendered a two-run Wall ball single to Victor Martinez. Morales was removed and showered with boos. Brandon Workman came on and got out of the jam on a double-play grounder (featuring a hideous bellyflop by the blundering Fielder) and a strikeout.

After he was burned by his bullpen in Game 2, Scherzer was in no mood to come out of this one. He put two men on to start the sixth, but retired three straight as the Sox stranded runners on second and third.

Tiger manager Jim Leyland hooked his starter after Scherzer yielded a near home run (less than a foot from the top of the Wall) to Gomes and walked the redoubtable Bogaerts with one out in the seventh. Then Ellsbury hit a grounder up the middle that was gloved, then dropped by stylemaster Iglesias.

Enter Victorino.

Don't worry about a thing. 'Cause every little thing gonna be all right.

what was that?

BY DAN SHAUGHNESSY • Globe Staff

CLOSE YOUR EYES AND IT IS 2004 ALL OVER AGAIN.

Tom Brady is throwing last-second touchdown passes en route to a certain Super Bowl, David Ortiz is the greatest clutch hitter in baseball history, and the unwashed Red Sox are escaping from a hopeless deficit while Mayor Menino is pumping tires on the duck boats.

What might be the most exciting day in Boston sports history ended at festive Fenway on Oct. 13 at 11:44 p.m., when Jarrod Saltalamacchia singled to left, scoring Jonny Gomes from third to give the Red Sox an impossible 6-5, series-squaring, come-from-behind victory over the stunned Detroit Tigers.

In the day of all days, the moment of all moments was the Ruthian sight of Ortiz crushing a first-pitch, game-tying grand slam off Tigers closer Joaquin Benoit in the eighth inning. As right fielder Torii Hunter flipped over the bullpen wall in fruitless pursuit of the flying seed, a Boston bullpen cop signaled "touchdown" and Fenway came to life.

This was not a walkoff. This was a liftoff. Flat on the ground for almost 17 strikeout-filled innings, Boston's championship hopes were launched into the airspace over the Back Bay as 38,029 fans rattled Fenway's 101-year-old timbers.

As Ortiz has been known to say, "This is our [expletive] city!"

"As we've seen, we're going to play to the final out," said Sox manager John Farrell. "David has come up big so many times in the postseason, none bigger than tonight. Just an incredible comeback here."

"We needed it, man," said Ortiz. "I tried not to do too much. I wasn't trying to hit a grand slam. Just try to put a good swing on the ball."

It was a Fisk-like moment.

Incredible? Unbelievable? Cosmic? Epic? Go ahead. Choose your word. This was right up there with any of the thrills we've seen at the ancient yard over the last century. Dave Roberts was summoned for the ceremonial first pitch and the event unfolded in a fashion reminiscent of the comeback against the Yankees in 2004.

In Foxborough or at Fenway, this was not a day to leave early.

All hope seemed lost on Yawkey Way. The Sox were striking out at a record pace — 17 times in a 1-0 defeat on Saturday and 13 more times in Game 2 as they fell behind, 5-1, through seven innings.

We were set to bury them. The Sox managed only one hit over the first 14 innings of the series. It was time for the fuzzy fellows to get out the razors. They were about to go down, two games to none, and face Justin Verlander in Game 3 in Detroit two days later. After not losing four straight games all season, the Sox looked like candidates for a sweep in the ALCS.

"We felt we were going to break out of it," said Saltalamacchia.

After Shane Victorino broke up Max Scherzer's no-hitter in the sixth, Dustin Pedroia broke the interminable Boston drought with an RBI double to left. Pedroia is the guy who was still playing with a broken bone in his hand at the end of the hideous 2012 season. He was embarrassed by the franchise's worst season in 47 years and he will never forget. Ortiz is the modern-day Bambino of this lovable nine, but Pedroia is the everyday player who sets the tone for the everyday miracles.

It was still 5-1 in the eighth when Tigers manager Jim Leyland got a little too cute and started a Joe Maddonesque parade of relievers. He wound up with big, nasty Benoit facing Ortiz with the bases loaded and two outs. Ortiz had already fanned twice on the night.

Papi struck on the first pitch. There was little doubt as his heat-seeking missile screeched toward the Sox bullpen. Hunter hit the wall at full speed and flipped as the ball soared beyond his reach. It was 5-5. It was already over.

"I know he has a good split-finger," said Ortiz. "I faced him a couple of times during the regular season."

Koji Uehara came on in the ninth and stuffed the already beaten Tigers. Then Rick Porcello came in to play the foil. Gomes hit a grounder to the left side and made it all the way to second on a throwing error by former Red Sox shortstop Jose Iglesias. He took third on a wild pitch and scored when Salty cracked his single to left. There was Ned Martinesque "pandemonium on the field," and the series was even.

Jarrod Saltalamacchia celebrates after slapping the single into left field that won Game 2 of the ALCS.

1-0

LACKEY VS VERLANDER

Mike Napoli of the Red Sox rounds the bases as Tigers pitcher Justin Verlander walks back to the mound after allowing Napoli's solo seventh-inning home run that stood up for the victory, thanks to John Lackey (right) and three relievers, who blanked Detroit on six hits. "You absolutely tip your hat to Verlander," said Jonny Gomes. "He pitched a heck of a game, but I think we can talk about John Lackey a little bit, too."

7-3

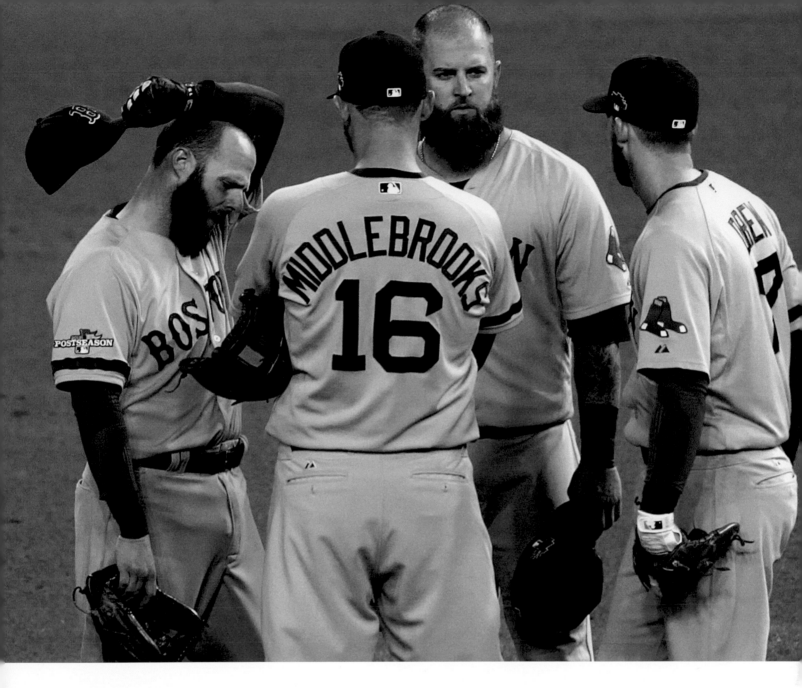

ALCS 4

PEAVY VS FISTER

Red Sox starter Jake Peavy appeared shellshocked after leaving the game in the fourth inning, having allowed seven runs on five hits and three walks. "I just couldn't make that big pitch to minimize the damage," he said. Red Sox infielders (above), awaiting a pitching change, and their mates had 12 hits — including four from Jacoby Ellsbury — but went 2-for-16 with runners in scoring position.

4-3

ALDS G5

LESTER VS SANCHEZ
Detroit catcher Alex Avila shows the ball after a second-inning collision with Boston's David Ross. The Red Sox jumped to a 4-0 lead, including Mike Napoli's second-inning homer, and got alert baserunning from Will Middlebrooks, as they held on to capture Game 5 behind another strong bullpen effort. It was the fourth one-run game in this ALCS, tying the record set in 1997.

5-2

A L D S [**6**]

BUCHHOLZ VS SCHERZER

Shane Victorino, who had been mired in a 2-for-23 slump in the ALCS, sent a 0-2 curveball from Detroit's Jose Veras into the Green Monster seats for his second career postseason grand slam, propelling the Red Sox into the World Series. Boston had fallen behind, 2-1, in the sixth inning, but Jonny Gomes doubled, Xander Bogaerts walked, and an error by Detroit's Jose Iglasias set up the series clincher. "It was a special moment. It's been a special year," said Victorino.

#POSTSEASON

Koji Uehara, the MVP of the series, celebrates after earning one win and three saves. The Sox closer pitched six shutout innings, fanning eight, allowing four hits and walking none.

BY PETER ABRAHAM • Globe Staff

fan boys

It's one, two, three strikes you're out at the old ballgame. But that's really not so bad these days. The strikeout, once something hitters did all they could to avoid, now has a degree of respect within baseball.

Though the Red Sox set a franchise record with 1,308 strikeouts during the regular season, they also led the majors in scoring by wearing down opposing pitchers with long, patient at-bats. Strikeouts, hitting coach Greg Colbrunn explained, are a cost of doing business.

"There's an awareness of pitch counts and starting pitchers sticking to a pitch count. So when guys go up there and battle for six or seven pitches, a strikeout is a good at-bat," Colbrunn said. "I know how that sounds, but it's true."

The Red Sox and many other teams are willing to accept high strikeout totals if their hitters are disciplined at the plate and, when they do connect with the ball, provide the home-run hitting power that is so difficult to find in baseball's post-steroids era.

Strikeout totals have risen for four consecutive years in the American League, climbing from 19.6 percent of the at-bats in 2010 to 21.9 percent this season. But the number of runs scored and home runs hit have risen, too.

Twenty-one players in baseball this season hit at least 25 home runs while striking out 100 or more times.

Seven were selected to the All-Star team. Strikeouts aren't quite cool, but they are accepted.

"You'd prefer somebody hit for power and not strike out often," Sox assistant general manager Mike Hazen said. "But those guys are the superstars and they're fairly rare. Sometimes you have to have an appreciation for what a good strikeout can do. You have to look at those long at-bats as contributing to the overall good of the lineup. Power is hard to find and you learn to live with the strikeouts."

Red Sox first baseman Mike Napoli is a good example of the tradeoff teams make. Napoli set a team record with 187 strikeouts this season. But he also contributed 38 doubles, 23 home runs, 92 RBIs, and 73 walks to the offense.

"I wish I didn't strike out as much as I do. It's embarrassing," Napoli said. "But I don't feel like I'm really helping the team if I get defensive at the plate and cut down on my swing. I have to do what I do."

Napoli struck out on three pitches only 17 times all season. On 120 occasions, he saw at least five pitches before striking out, and there were 17 times he saw seven or more pitches before going down. He averaged 4.59 pitches per plate appearance, the best in the majors.

The postseason offers an even clearer view of how a hitter such as Napoli can be frustrating and fruitful at the same time. He struck out 15 times in his first 33 postseason at-bats this year. But Napoli's home run in Game 3 of the American League Championship Series was the difference in a 1-0 victory. Napoli then homered and doubled to help win Game 5 against the Detroit Tigers.

"He goes up there and very rarely does he have a short at-bat," Colbrunn said. "There's a lot of merit to that. Mike is a threat every time he goes up to the plate."

Colbrunn played in the majors from 1992-2004. He has watched what he calls a "culture shift" when it comes to strikeouts.

"When I first came up you were supposed to put the ball in play with two strikes," he said. "Certain hitters struck out 100 times, but not too many. Now you look at some of the best hitters in the game and they are guys who strike out a lot."

The 10 hitters with the most strikeouts in baseball this season averaged 32 home runs and 92 RBIs.

For Napoli, it's a matter of maintaining his confidence.

"When I strike out I'm not going back to the dugout with my head down," he said. "I have to be ready to go back up there again later in the game and give a good at-bat. I know what my approach is and I'm going to stick to it. I might miss some pitches. But something good is going to come from it when I get one."

DIVISION

THE SOX DEFEATED
THE RAYS TO RETURN
TO THE ALCS FOR THE
FIRST TIME SINCE
2008, WHEN THEY
LOST TO TAMPA BAY IN
SEVEN GAMES.

REMATCH

Game 1 starter Jon Lester worked on his footwork.

12-2 TB | 0 1 0 | 1 0 0 | 0 0 0 | **2** 4 0
BOS | 0 0 0 | 5 3 0 | 0 4 x | **12** 14 0
GAME 1 FRIDAY 10/4/2013 • FENWAY PARK ooooo

7-4 TB | 0 1 0 | 0 2 1 | 0 0 0 | **4** 8 2
BOS | 2 0 2 | 1 1 0 | 0 1 x | **7** 11 0
GAME 2 SATURDAY 10/5/2013 • FENWAY PARK ooooo

5-4 BOS | 1 0 0 | 0 2 0 | 0 0 1 | **4** 7 0
TB | 0 0 0 | 0 3 0 | 0 1 1 | **5** 11 1
GAME 3 MONDAY 10/7/2013 • TROPICANA FIELD ooooo

3-1 BOS | 0 0 0 | 0 0 0 | 2 0 1 | **3** 6 0
TB | 0 0 0 | 0 0 1 | 0 0 0 | **1** 6 0
GAME 4 TUESDAY 10/8/2013 • TROPICANA FIELD ooooo

VS TAMPA BAY

BY PETER ABRAHAM • Globe Staff

IN THIS MOST SURPRISING of Red Sox seasons, the Sox headed to the American League Championship Series after beating the Tampa Bay Rays, 3-1, in a hard-fought Game 4 at Tropicana Field in St. Petersburg, Fla. » The Red Sox easily dispatched the Rays in the first two games of the best-of-five Division Series at Fenway Park. But the two games on the road were tense, nail-biting affairs. » After losing, 5-4, on a walkoff home run in Game 3, the Sox held the Rays to one run on six hits in Game 4. Craig Breslow worked 1⅓ innings for the win. Junichi Tazawa got one out in the eighth inning before Koji Uehara got the final four outs for his second save of the series. » It was Uehara who had allowed Jose Lobaton's game-winning home run in Game 3. » "I wasn't down on myself at all," Uehara said. "Whatever the results were, I had the confidence for this game." » Red Sox manager John Farrell managed the bullpen to near perfection as the three relievers pitched 3⅓ scoreless innings, allowing one hit and striking out seven without a walk. » Shane Victorino and Dustin Pedroia had RBI singles for the Sox. Rookie Xander Bogaerts came off the bench and scored two runs after drawing walks. » "That's the kind of thing you look back on and talk about, executing and doing the little things," Victorino said. » Tampa Bay used nine pitchers but was unable to stave off elimination for the fifth time in 10 days. The Sox outscored the Rays, 26-12, in the series. » "They were really good," Rays manager Joe Maddon said. "They didn't make any mistakes. You could see their grit. I talked about that from spring training on. I think they really promoted the character from within that group and they're just gamers." » The postgame celebration was a bit calmer than the one after the Red Sox clinched the American League East. The players did dump a tub of ice water on Farrell and soaked general manager Ben Cherington › PAGE 61

Red Sox manager John Farrell hugs closer Koji Uehara after Uehara rebounded from a rocky Game 3 effort to finish off the Rays in the Game 4 clincher.

12-2

ALDS 1

LESTER VS MOORE

Jonny Gomes scores from second on Stephen Drew's infield hit as the Red Sox take command with a five-run fourth inning. All nine Boston batters had at least one hit and one run in the game, just the third time that's been done in postseason history, and the first time since 1936. Jon Lester allowed three hits and two runs in 7⅔ innings.

FROM 58 • with champagne. Before they celebrated, the Red Sox had to overcome a 1-0 deficit through six innings of Game 4, with the possibility of a winner-take-all Game 5 against Rays' ace David Price.

Tampa Bay starter Jeremy Hellickson was 2-6 with a 7.02 earned run average in his last 10 appearances of the regular season and hadn't pitched since Sept. 27. He retired the Sox in order in the first inning on 12 pitches.

But Hellickson walked David Ortiz and Mike Napoli on eight pitches to start the second inning, getting righthander Jamey Wright up in the Tampa Bay bullpen.

When Daniel Nava singled to right field to load the bases, Maddon had a quicker hook than Marvelous Marvin Hagler and went to Wright.

Wright struck out Jarrod Saltalamacchia looking at a 2-and-2 curveball. Stephen Drew was next and he lined a cutter to the right side of the diamond. First baseman James Loney made a leaping catch for the second out, then fired to second base to catch Napoli and end the inning. Through six innings, the Red Sox were 1 for 5 with runners in scoring position and had stranded six runners.

Maddon went to lefthander Jake McGee for the seventh. That's when Farrell started making his moves.

Jonny Gomes pinch hit for Saltalamacchia and he flied to center. Bogaerts, whom Farrell elected not to use against McGee in Game 3, pinch hit for Drew and walked.

"I reserve the right to change my mind," Farrell said. "I felt like at that moment, as tough as lefthanders have been on Stephen, we had to try something different."

Middlebrooks struck out, but Ellsbury singled and Bogaerts went to third.

With Victorino up, Maddon called in righthander Joel Peralta. His first pitch was a curveball that bounced away from Lobaton and Bogaerts scored. Ellsbury, who was stealing second on the pitch, kept on going to third base. > PAGE 64

61

7-4

A L D S

VS PRICE

Shane Victorino and Tampa Bay's Ben Zobrist get tangled up at second base as Victorino spoils a potential double-play ball, allowing Jacoby Ellsbury to score for Boston. Ellsbury had three hits and three runs, and David Ortiz homered twice off David Price — who had allowed just two homers all season to lefty hitters — as Boston seized a 2-0 series lead.

FROM 61 • That proved to be a smart play as Victorino's infield single scored Ellsbury and the Sox had a 2-1 lead. Pedroia followed with a single before Ortiz struck out.

The Sox added a run in the ninth when Bogaerts walked and eventually scored on a sacrifice fly by Pedroia.

"I tried to stay calm and stay with my approach. Walks are fine," Bogaerts said. "I thought there was a possibility that I would hit. It worked out well."

Jake Peavy had not pitched since Sept. 25. The veteran righthander savored the chance to take the mound in the postseason and at least partially erase the memory of two poor Division Series starts for the Padres in 2005 and '06.

Peavy was brilliant for five innings this time, shutting out the Rays on three hits and only 56 pitches. But his teammates provided no run support.

Yunel Escobar doubled to start the sixth inning, took third on a groundout, and scored when David DeJesus singled to right field. One out later with lefthanded hitting James Loney up, Farrell called in Breslow.

Peavy, who had thrown only 74 pitches, walked off the mound staring straight ahead. Breslow struck out Loney and the Sox were down, 1-0. The bullpen strangled the Rays from there.

A L D S 3

BUCHHOLZ VS COBB
Mike Napoli salutes Dustin Pedroia after Pedroia's RBI groundout made it 4-4 in the ninth inning, but the Rays' Jose Lobaton blasted a walkoff homer off Sox closer Koji Uehara (right) in the bottom of the inning to win it. The Rays trailed, 3-0, before Evan Longoria's fifth-inning three-run homer tied it, and an eighth-inning RBI groundout put them ahead.

5-4

3-1

A L D S 4

PEAVY VS HELLICKSON

Trailing 1-0 through six innings, the Red Sox uncharacteristically manufactured two runs on a walk, a single, a steal, a wild pitch and a two-out infield hit by Shane Victorino (above), which scored Jacoby Ellsbury with the eventual winning run. Boston's bullpen was brilliant (3⅓ innings, one hit, seven strikeouts) in relief of Jake Peavy as the Red Sox advanced to the ALCS.

BY PETER ABRAHAM • Globe Staff

chin up

When the Red Sox held "Beard Night" in September and filled every seat at Fenway Park, Mike Napoli and Jonny Gomes joked that they should ask the team for a share of the profits. Back in spring training, when Gomes showed up with scraggly whiskers and Napoli decided he would stop shaving just for kicks, nobody guessed that baseball players with hairy faces would become a cottage industry complete with T-shirts and posters.

But the thing about the beards that gets missed is that it's not really about the beards. It's about what they represent.

For the better part of two years, playing for the Red Sox had become a chore. The September collapse in 2011 led to the team losing 93 games in 2012. Most every move the Sox made failed, particularly the hiring of unpopular manager Bobby Valentine.

The enduring image of last season was a photograph of Josh Beckett, Adrian Gonzalez, and Nick Punto smiling as a private jet whisked them away from Boston after they were traded to the Los Angeles Dodgers.

The Dodgers trade helped general manager Ben Cherington renovate the roster with players who would improve the talent level of the team and change the Eeyore attitude of the clubhouse. But until the group assembled in spring training, the chemistry component was uncertain.

"Every team needs something," Gomes said. "We all knew what the big picture was, what we were trying to do. But there had to be something to bring people together." Gomes was on playoff teams in Tampa Bay (2008), Cincinnati (2010), and Oakland (2012). In all three cases, teams with losing records the previous year became winners. Gomes noticed that all three teams had little rituals that helped the players bond.

"That stuff is totally irrelevant to baseball," he said. "But if everybody gets on the same page, maybe it does help. Good teams seem to have certain music or ways they celebrate. Quirky things can bring people together."

So when Napoli started growing a beard, Dustin Pedroia and David Ross joined him, as did others. Manager John Farrell, smooth of chin all his life, never raised an objection.

"It's a signature for this team," he said. "It's a bonding element. You have to have ways to have fun sometimes. It takes the focus off the daily grind."

The beards might have vanished had the Red Sox started slowly. But winning 12 of the first 16 games almost mandated that no changes would be made.

The team further bonded on April 15, the unforgettable day of the Boston Marathon bombings. After winning a game against Tampa Bay at Fenway Park, the Sox boarded a flight to Cleveland to start a road trip. That night, as news of the tragedy spread, about 20 players gathered for dinner, an unusually large group. The following day in the dugout, they hung a jersey with "617" on the back in support of the victims. For Farrell, that moment was telling.

"We saw some things come out of the individuals that spoke to their understanding that they were in a special place and showed some character at a very difficult and unique time," he said. "Whether that was the galvanizing moment for this team, I can't say that. But it was a moment in time where guys showed a different side of them, that this was a special group."

The Sox never faltered, staying in first place for the bulk of the season. For the first time since 2009, they headed back to the postseason — bearded. Even babyfaced holdouts like Jacoby Ellsbury, Stephen Drew, and Daniel Nava eventually joined in.

Many of the players also have three lines shaved into the back of their heads by a clubhouse barber, a style usually favored by high school kids.

"It's been a blast. This is the most fun I've ever had playing baseball," Jarrod Saltalamacchia said. "It's not because of me doing well. What's great about this team is we root for the next guy. The beards are just part of it."

tall tale

BY ANTHONY GULIZIA • Globe Correspondent

Hours before the start of most home games, Yawkey Way is bustling with fans. Navigating the crowd that fills the narrow street outside Fenway Park is often difficult, but standing nearly 10 feet above the pavement definitely improves your sight lines.

That's the vantage point of Big League Brian, a.k.a. Brian Dwyer, better recognized as the "man on the stilts." Dressed in white baseball pants and a Red Sox jersey, he is hard to miss. As he works his way through the crowd, Dwyer poses for pictures and catches up with frequent visitors.

"They love to check in, they love to say hi and talk for a moment," Dwyer said. "I represent a tangible, approachable part of Fenway for them."

When John Henry purchased the Red Sox in 2002, a series of renovations unfolded and by the end of that season, the Yawkey Way concourse opened for entertainment before the games. A string of former Faneuil Hall street performers began working the area when it opened, and Dwyer sought a way to stand out, quite literally.

"I decided to get on stilts, we had so many performers and I wanted to do something different," said Dwyer, who is 5 feet, 8 inches with his feet on the ground. "I already had really good balance and coordination, and the first time I got up on stilts, it was just fine."

WE HAD SO MANY PERFORMERS AND I WANTED TO DO SOMETHING DIFFERENT. BRIAN DWYER

There aren't as many performers on Yawkey Way now, but there is never a shortage of fun. Dwyer, who wears a righthanded first baseman's mitt, plays catch with young fans and delivers quirky one-liners to keep the mood light before the game. When he wants to get the attention of the crowd, he turns to his signature trick: He balances his hat on his nose, and after a few seconds, flips it back to the top of his head. Often, he improvises to suit the crowd's mood.

"Comedy, a lot of silent comedy, just looks and takes and faces, it's all what the situation calls for," Dwyer said. "Sometimes, I'll bring out the ukelele and sing 'Take Me Out to the Ball Game.'" Or accompany the Hot Tamales, a brass band that provides live music for the crowd. He bounces his baseball off the band's snare drum in between drummer hits — a perfectly timed trick that has been carefully crafted over his 12 seasons of entertaining on Yawkey Way.

"It's a riot," said Matt Pellerin, a fan from Manchester, N.H. "He's the first thing you see, he's exciting and he goes crazy with everybody, I love it."

Dwyer, a Somerville native, attended Ringling Bros. and Barnum & Bailey Clown College and toured with the Cole Bros. Circus of the Stars for four years. He has only fallen twice in his career as a stilt walker. One tumble came at a photo shoot on a friend's stilts, which had frayed straps. The other time, he was at Fenway after the 2004 World Series victory and was walking through the concrete hallway when he slipped in a puddle of cooking oil.

"I didn't know it because the lights weren't on," Dwyer recalled. "And I was like Bambi on ice."

Even so, Dwyer said he was most worried when, during either the 2004 or 2007 World Series, roughly 30 riot squad officers marched down Yawkey Way.

"It was getting close to game time, and SWAT people ran in a straight line, and jogged down the street," Dwyer said. "Full riot gear. I think they wanted to just have a presence, but out of nowhere, 30 guys jogging down the middle of the street and I'm thinking, 'Is there something I need to know?'

"I'm not in a very advantageous position if anything is going wrong."

But more often than not, Dwyer holds the best position, and that's perched above the crowd.

SEASON

THE RED SOX MADE A 28-GAME IMPROVEMENT FROM 69-93 TO 97-65, THE TEAM'S LARGEST NON-STRIKE SEASON REBOUND IN 67 YEARS.

REDEMPTION

Red Sox stretch out before the exhibition season opener at JetBlue Park.

2012
AMERICAN LEAGUE EAST

	W	L	%	GB
New York	95	67	.586	
Baltimore	93	69	.574	2
Tampa Bay	90	72	.556	5
Toronto	73	89	.451	22
Boston	**69**	**93**	**.426**	26

2013
AMERICAN LEAGUE EAST

	W	L	%	GB
Boston	**97**	**65**	**.599**	
Tampa Bay	92	71	.564	5.5
Baltimore	85	77	.525	12
New York	85	77	.525	12
Toronto	74	88	.457	23

APRIL

18-8

The Red Sox raced ahead in the AL East, thanks to a combined 9-0 month from Buchholz and Lester and a late boost from Ortiz, who batted .500 with 15 RBI in nine games after missing the first 15.

MAY

15-15

The Sox never lost more than three straight all year, but they had their worst stretch of the season in mid-May, dropping nine of 11. They ended the month one game up in the division at 33-23.

JUNE

17-11

The Red Sox straddled June and July with an 8-1 home stand that included two wins and four saves from Uehara, who established himself as the closer in the wake of injuries to Hanrahan and Bailey.

JULY

15-10

After holding down first place for two months, the Sox briefly slipped behind Tampa Bay in late July, but they swept Seattle for their MLB-leading 22nd series victory to regain the division lead.

Dustin Pedroia warms up at JetBlue Park in Fort Myers, Fla.

AUGUST

16-12

Pitching helped the Sox take control of the division, as they allowed 3 runs or fewer and 8 hits or fewer in 11 straight games from Aug. 19-31 – the longest such streak in MLB since Toronto in 1991.

SEPTEMBER

16-9

The Sox averaged 6.48 runs a game in September, their highest average for the month since 1938. They also tied St. Louis for baseball's best record and led the AL for the first time since 1986.

BY RON DRISCOLL • Globe Correspondent

RELENTLESS. The word probably elicited more than a few smirks on Opening Day 2013 at Yankee Stadium, after the Red Sox had defeated New York 8-2. Boston was coming off an abysmal 2012 season, its worst in 47 years, and new manager John Farrell had the apparent chutzpah to intimate that his players had already moved on from that train wreck of a season. ❯❯ "There's tremendous energy with this group," said Farrell. "The one word we continue to talk about in here is to be relentless." ❯❯ On that day, Farrell was referring to Jonny Gomes hustling to score all the way from second base on an infield hit. And even as Boston fans and foes kept waiting for the other shoe to drop and the season to turn sour, the Red Sox exhibited that relentless nature. They started off 12-4, while helping buoy the city in the wake of the Marathon bombings. They turned the tables on their archrivals, dominating the Yankees with a 13-6 record in their season series, and they developed a penchant for grinding out at-bats, come-from-behind rallies and walkoff victories. ❯❯ The Sox proceeded to hold down first place in the AL East for all but 19 days of the season. When Tampa Bay pulled even with them at the top of the division in late August, the Red Sox ran away and hid by taking 17 out of 21. ❯❯ They provided a metaphor for the season on Aug. 1: first they finished off a 15-inning walkoff victory over the visiting Mariners in the early morning, then stunned them by tallying six runs in the bottom of the ninth for an 8-7 win before the night was out. "We just play until they tell us we can't," said Dustin Pedroia, who proceeded to dub Boston #WalkOffCity on Twitter. ❯❯ "There's no quit in this bunch," said Farrell after the improbable rally against Seattle. "They truly believe there's a chance to do something special, whether it's on a given night or over the course of a given year. That one would be this year." ❯❯ The Year of the Relentless Red Sox.

Mike Napoli comes in for a landing on home plate after hitting a walk-off home run in the 11th inning to beat the Yankees, 8-7, on July 21.

RED SOX
YANKEES

APR 1

As the scoreboard shows, the season is already off to a good start when Red Sox rookie left fielder Jackie Bradley Jr. makes a leaping catch to end the third inning of Boston's 8-2 rout of the Yankees. Bradley walked three times and scored twice, while Jon Lester outdueled C.C. Sabathia as John Farrell won his Red Sox managerial debut.

BY BOB RYAN • Globe Correspondent

THESE ARE THE VERY BEST SEASONS, THE ONES THAT EXCEED OUR EXPECTATIONS.

Nobody was prepared for the exquisite adventure that was the 1967 pennant race. Actually being part of a pennant race was a thrill in and of itself.

Unlike 1967, there was no need for final-day drama this year. The 2013 Red Sox took charge of the AL East in early September, whereas on Oct. 1, 1967, there was a very real possibility it would be the last day of the season, period. We were deprived of the suspense and excitement generated by the events of that day, but in its place is the satisfaction of a season during which baseball dignity was restored here in Boston.

What were the expectations when the 2013 season began?

The team simply had to be better. The 2012 Red Sox were bad, but they were not 69-93 bad. It was a perfect storm of negativity, combining injuries (David Ortiz, Jacoby Ellsbury), poor pitching, and what might have been the worst managing job seen in the major leagues in the last 130 years.

But they play in the American League East. Toronto appeared to be loaded. The Yankees were old, 'tis true, but in most cases they were distinguished elders worthy of professional respect. The Orioles figured to have something of a market correction after all those one-run triumphs, but they were going to be quite respectable. And Tampa

Bay had all that pitching. To me, 81-81 would have constituted reasonable improvement.

The important thing was to fumigate the premises, to make fans believe that the events of September 2011 and all of 2012 were aberrational and not the new norm on Yawkey Way. Basic credibility had to be restored. Winning the AL East was not required.

Ben Cherington gets a lot of the credit, but I'm sure he'd be the first to tell you any general manager would rather be lucky than good. The baseball consensus was that he overpaid for the likes of Shane Victorino, Jonny Gomes, and Mike Napoli — of course, you don't hear any of that now that each man has come through. Give Cherington credit for identifying just the right personalities to brighten up the clubhouse, in addition to bringing specific talents to the playing field. Ben was 3 for 3 with these guys. Two out of three would have been a passing GM grade.

And then there is the wondrous Mr. Uehara.

As everyone knows by now, he was not brought here to be the closer. He only became the ninth-inning guy after both Joel Hanrahan and Andrew Bailey went down. Serendipity reigns in this regard.

Let me note, however, that the idea of Uehara having some measure of

success is not a shock to baseball's more seasoned observers. In Sports Illustrated's baseball preview issue, an anonymous rival scout said of Uehara: "He just knows how to mess up bat speeds, never walks anybody. A very underappreciated player."

Not anymore.

By way of amplification, the author of the SI Red Sox preview had this to say: "Uehara may be the steal of the winter, coming off a year in which he struck out 43 batters and walked three for the Rangers." The Red Sox were picked to go 75-87 and finish last in the division.

It's almost ridiculous how well everything worked out for the Red Sox. Gomes and Stephen Drew each got off to slow starts. But we don't mind seeing either of them up in key situations now, do we? It has been a real tag-team deal offensively, with guys dovetailing their contributions as the season unfolded.

The beard thing is their shtick, and that's fine. Gimmicks are nice. Just let me remind you that winning begets camaraderie, not the other way around. They have won all these games — not because they have bonded over beards, or anything else — but because they have played winning baseball, which in this day-to-day grind of a sport in which people spend so much time together means not bitching when your 0 for 4 coincides with a victory.

APR 1 5

Red Sox reliever Koji Uehara returns to the dugout after retiring the Rays in the top of the eighth inning on Patriots Day, then Mike Napoli doubles home Dustin Pedroia for a 2-1 victory and a three-game sweep.

Scenes from the aftermath of the Boston Marathon bombings are displayed on the Fenway Park center-field message board before the April 20 game between the Red Sox and the Royals.

BY JULIAN BENBOW • Globe Staff

THE EMOTIONS HAD BEEN BOILING ALL WEEK. A FIVE-DAY STRETCH THAT HAD BEEN FRANTIC AND UNSETTLING HAD COME TO AN END.

So had the search for the suspected perpetrators of the bombings that shook the city.

Looking out at the faces in the crowd, people who had come to Fenway Park to escape, to celebrate, and recapture some of the normalcy they had lost, David Ortiz felt what they were feeling.

"This past week, I don't think there was one human being who wasn't affected by what we got going on down here," Ortiz said. "This past week for me, myself, I was very emotional and angry about the whole situation and got to get that out of my chest and make sure our fans and everyone in the nation knows that this is a great nation and part of it was supporting each other when everything went down."

At the end of the ceremony that preceded Boston's 4-3 win over Kansas City on April 20, Ortiz's microphone was hot and his words were clear:

"This is our [expletive] city, and nobody is going to dictate our freedom. Stay strong."

He later apologized for the swear, but not the sentiment. But in the wake of incomprehensible terror, the words were forceful, defiant, and proud.

"I'm from the Dominican Republic and the one thing that I always say is me and my family are blessed by being in this country," Ortiz said. "And I love this country and I would do anything for this country. Everybody was one unit and that's what matters."

Preaching the mantra "Boston Strong," the Red Sox took the first steps in helping an embattled city to heal. The team's support added to the solidarity the city had shown all week in the face of tragedy.

Governor Deval Patrick said, "The response of the people in the crowd in the stadium has been the response of people all over the Commonwealth all week and, frankly, all over the world."

Over the course of the pregame ceremony, emotions swung from moment to moment.

A montage played on the outfield scoreboards, image after powerful image. Marathon volunteers lined the Green Monster in front of an American flag as wide as the 231-foot long wall. The Royals and Red Sox stood shoulder to shoulder along the foul lines.

"Guys were fighting back tears on the line," said Sox reliever Andrew Bailey. "I've never been a part of something like that."

For the national anthem, the crowd of 35,152 sang out in unison.

The field was flooded with the faces they had seen endlessly on television over the past four days. Patrick, Boston Police commissioner Edward Davis, and FBI special agent Richard DesLauriers. They joined marathoners Rick Hoyt and his father Dick, longtime symbols of the sacrifice and resilience, who threw out the ceremonial first pitch along with off-duty firefighter Matt Patterson and bombing victim Steven Byrne.

Thinking about pitching was almost impossible for starter Clay Buchholz with everything unfolding in front of him.

"I don't think I would've been able to watch it and pitch at the same time," he said. "That was my frame of mind going in. That's the part that I wanted to get through."

One minute everyone in the ballpark was silent, remembering the victims. The next they were applauding the heroes in front of them on the field.

To be able to play, the day after a manhunt left the city all but frozen, was a statement in itself. Security was heightened. Earlier in the day, police dogs checked the ballpark. Officers in bright yellow jackets seemed to be at every turn. Fans were wanded down at the entrances.

But there were signs that the day obviously meant more.

It took a 4:30 a.m. flight for Neil Diamond to make it to Boston from Los Angeles. Then, he called into the main Fenway Park switchboard and asked if he could sing "Sweet Caroline." The crowd was his choir.

BY DAVID FILIPOV AND MARIA CRAMER • Globe Staff

FROM THE START OF THIS UNLIKELY SEASON, THE BOSTON RED SOX HAVE BEEN INEXTRICABLY LINKED WITH THE BOSTON MARATHON BOMBINGS.

The blasts at the finish line detonated minutes after the final pitch of the 3-2 Red Sox victory in the traditional Patriots Day game. It was star slugger David Ortiz who coined Boston's memorable, expletive-pierced rallying cry. The Boston Strong logo borrowed the Gothic "B" that adorns the team's caps.

And Fenway Park became the venue where, throughout the summer, crowds cheered the victims and the healers as they walked — or were helped — to the mound for the ceremonial first pitch.

As this bearded band of ballplayers progressed, its rise from last place to the World Series took on a deeper meaning in a city rising from one of the most shockingly violent episodes in its history. Boston needed the Red Sox a bit more than usual this year, as a distraction, a measure of comfort, and a unifying force. And more than ever, the team took on the personality of its recovering city.

"There is a magic to this team," said Dan Lebowitz, executive director of the Center for the Study of Sport in Society at Northeastern University. "The Marathon happens, it was so injurious to the city … and the next thing you know there's this team of destiny rising through the ashes. It creates this dynamic of hope for the city moving forward."

Like the New Orleans Saints team that brought a Super Bowl victory to a city devastated by Hurricane Katrina, or the New York Yankees' World Series run a few weeks after the Sept. 11 terrorist attacks, this year's Red Sox embodied the way sport can bring together a community sundered by disaster. Even a nation, at times, united to the strains of "Sweet Caroline" in ballparks across the country.

It started with the Red Sox jersey reading "Boston Strong" with the city's 617 area code the Sox hung in their dugout for a 7-2 win in Cleveland the night after the bombing. A gesture that, according to team executive vice president Charles Steinberg, was initiated by the players.

But as the season progressed, and as the team defied predictions of mediocrity and its personality started coming through, fans recognized attributes New Englanders have always embraced: the almost stubborn adherence to a team's patient strategy of driving up pitch counts, the unbridled, genuine enthusiasm of the players, and, of course, an uncanny ability to grind out wins against the odds.

Even those most deeply affected by the bombings found in the team a welcome distraction from the grim aftermath of the bombings, which killed three people and wounded more than 260. An MIT police officer was killed three days later, allegedly by the bombing suspects.

"A world championship isn't going to undo anything that's happened, but it's good for the family to be living through something that's an exciting time in our community," said Larry Marchese, spokesman for the Richard family of Dorchester, whose younger son was killed in the bombing and whose daughter lost a leg.

Members of the Red Sox say they have benefited from the city's resilience.

"It brought a closeness to me to the city, seeing how everybody rallied around each other," catcher David Ross told reporters.

"I do think these players feel a special bond and connection to this city," said team president Larry Lucchino. "As human beings, these guys understand what the city, the region, the victims went through and it helped them bond to each other and to this community."

Boston Marathon bombing victim Jeff Bauman threw out a ceremonial first pitch before the May 28 game against the Phillies.

The season included many tributes to first responders and victims of the Boston Marathon bombings. Players and fans take time out before a game against Kansas City on April 20 (page 86), which also saw a surprise appearance by Neil Diamond. On May 15, Boston EMTs watch a Marathon video presentation; on Aug. 26, firefighters are honored; and on Sept. 14, Sydney Corcoran and her mother Celeste throw out ceremonial first pitches (page 87).

David Ortiz exhorts the crowd before the game on April 20.

MAY 2 3

Terry Francona, who guided the Red Sox from 2004-11, returns to Fenway as the Indians' manager, and the Tribe clubs the Sox, 12-3. "You don't want to be the focus," said Francona of a between-innings video tribute he received. "But it felt good."

JUNE 1 8

Mike Napoli (left) and Jonny Gomes celebrate Gomes's walkoff two-run homer that gave Boston a 3-1 victory and a sweep of its day-night doubleheader with the Rays.

JULY 2 1

The Red Sox, including David Ortiz (34), who is trying to rip Mike Napoli's shirt off, mob Napoli as he crosses the plate in the 11th inning after a walkoff home run that gave Boston a 8-7 victory.

JULY 3 0

The Red Sox obtained Jake Peavy from the White Sox in a three-team, seven-player deal in which they gave up shortstop Jose Iglesias. Peavy went 4-1, including this seven-inning effort against Arizona in his Boston debut, which the Sox won, 5-2.

Dustin Pedroia (15) and Jonny Gomes celebrate the game-winning hit by Daniel Nava, which capped a six-run ninth inning and gave Boston an 8-7 victory over the Mariners. Trailing 7-1 after seven, it was the first time the Sox won a game they trailed by six as late as the eighth inning since July 3, 1940.

AUG 2 5

Red Sox starting pitcher Jake Peavy throws a complete-game three-hitter as the Red Sox blast the Dodgers, 8-1. Peavy improved to 14-2 against LA in 25 career starts and the Red Sox handed the Dodgers their first series loss in 18 series, a club record.

Clay Buchholz makes his first start in three months for Boston, pitching five shutout innings while allowing only three hits. He outdueled Tampa Bay ace David Price and improved to 10-0 as the Red Sox moved 8½ games ahead of the Rays in the AL East.

Pinch hitter Mike Carp hits the first pitch he sees for a grand slam in the 10th inning as the Sox earned a 7-3 victory against Tampa Bay. It was the first pinch-hit grand slam for the Sox since 2003. Koji Uehara extended his streak of consecutive batters retired to 34, a club record.

SEPT 1 5

Mariano Rivera of the Yankees salutes the crowd after he was honored before his final game at Fenway Park on Sept. 15. The Red Sox won, 9-2, to end the season with 13 victories in 19 games against the Yankees, their most wins in a season vs. New York in 40 years.

SEPT 2 0

Red Sox manager
John Farrell and
designated hitter
David Ortiz celebrate
Boston's AL East
pennant-clinching, 6-3
victory over Toronto.
Jon Lester went seven
strong innings for his
100th career victory.

DATE	OPPONENT	SCORE		PLACE			THE LOWDOWN
APRIL							
4/1	@ New York Yankees	W	8-2	1st	▲	.5	Ellsbury opens with three hits, drives in two.
4/3	@ New York Yankees	W	7-4	1st	▲	1	Buchholz allows one earned run in seven innings.
4/4	@ New York Yankees	L	4-2	T-1st	—		Pettitte goes eight strong, giving up one run.
4/5	@ Toronto	W	6-4	T-1st	—		Middlebrooks homers, Napoli drives in three.
4/6	@ Toronto	L	5-0	T-1st	—		Happ, Jays bullpen limit Sox to two hits.
4/7	@ Toronto	W	13-0	1st	▲	1	Middlebrooks blasts three of six Sox homers.
4/8	Baltimore	W	3-1	1st	▲	2	Buchholz dominant again: 7 IP, 0 ER, 8 K.
4/10	Baltimore	L	8-5	1st	▲	1	Machado ninth-inning homer wins it.
4/11	Baltimore	L	3-2	T-1st	—		Aceves (5 IP, 2 ER) gets no-decision in spot start.
4/13,	Tampa Bay,	W	2-1	1st	▲	.5	Victorino walk-off single scores Ellsbury in 10th.
4/14,	Tampa Bay,	W	5-0	1st	▲	1	Buchholz strikes out 11, gives up two hits in 8 IP.
4/15	Tampa Bay	W	3-2	1st	▲	1.5	Napoli double off Monster gives Sox another walk-off.
4/16	@ Cleveland	W	7-2	1st	▲	1.5	Sox score seven runs in second inning in first game vs. Francona.
4/17	@ Cleveland	W	6-3	1st	▲	1.5	Carp doubles twice, triples once, drives in three.
4/18	@ Cleveland	W	6-3	1st	▲	2.5	Lester strong and Bailey gets the save.
4/20	vs. Kansas City	W	4-3	1st	▲	2	Nava hits game-winning homer in first game at Fenway post-Marathon.
4/21	vs. Kansas City	L	4-2	1st	▲	1.5	Ortiz's three hits in second game of season not enough.
4/21	vs. Kansas City	L	5-4	1st	▲	1.5	Webster (6 IP, 3 ER) solid in major league debut.
4/22	Oakland	W	9-6	1st	▲	2	Napoli (double, grand slam) collects five RBIs.
4/23	Oakland	L	13-0	1st	▲	1	Colon dominant, Aceves not, in rain-shortened blowout.
4/24	Oakland	W	6-5	1st	▲	2	Bullpen is shaky, but Bailey strikes out the side in ninth.
4/25	Houston	W	7-2	1st	▲	2	Ortiz hits his first homer of the year; Buchholz goes 5-0.
4/26	Houston	W	7-3	1st	▲	2	Dempster strikes out 10 in six innings for first win of the season.
4/27	Houston	W	8-4	1st	▲	2	Ortiz's hot start continues with 2-for-3, 3-RBI effort.
4/28	Houston	W	6-1	1st	▲	2.5	Sox complete sweep behind Lackey's six innings of one-run ball.
4/30	@ Toronto	L	9-7	1st	▲	2	Encarnacion hits two homers, driving in four runs.
MAY							
5/1	@ Toronto	W	10-1	1st	▲	2	Buchholz lowers ERA to 1.01 with seven scoreless.
5/2	@ Toronto	W	3-1	1st	▲	2.5	Dempster strong again as four relievers throw three shutout innings.
5/3	@ Texas	L	7-0	1st	▲	2.5	Former Sox Beltre goes 4-for-5 with three RBIs.
5/4	@ Texas	L	5-1	1st	▲	1.5	Ogando scatters six hits, two walks in six innings.
5/5	@ Texas	L	4-3	1st	▲	1.5	Beltre (2-for-5) walks off against Mortensen.
5/6	Minnesota	W	6-5	1st	▲	2	Drew's walk-off double scores Saltalamacchia in the 11th.
5/7	Minnesota	L	6-1	1st	▲	1	Twins score four in eighth off Dempster, Breslow.
5/8	Minnesota	L	15-8	T-1st	—		Twins' seven-run second is the difference in a slugfest.
5/9	Minnesota	L	5-3	T-1st	—		Lackey (7 IP, 5 R, 1 ER) betrayed by defense.
5/10	Toronto	W	5-0	T-1st	—		Lester tosses one-hit complete game.
5/11	Toronto	L	3-2	2nd	▼	1	Lind homers off Tazawa in the ninth.
5/12	Toronto	L	12-4	3rd	▼	2	Bautista homers off Dempster, Mortensen.
5/14	@ Tampa Bay	L	5-3	3rd	▼	3	Rays get five runs off Lackey in fourth.
5/15	@ Tampa Bay	W	9-2	2nd	▼	2	Sox knock out Price in eight-run third.
5/16	@ Tampa Bay	W	4-3	2nd	▼	1	Middlebrooks's three-run double in ninth wins it.
5/17	@ Minnesota	W	3-2	2nd	▼	1	Gomes's sac fly in 10th gives Sox another narrow win.
5/18	@ Minnesota	W	12-5	2nd	▼	1	Ortiz homers twice and drives in six in laugher.
5/19	@ Minnesota	W	5-1	2nd	▼	.5	Pedroia two-run long ball in ninth provides insurance.
5/20	@ Chicago White Sox	L	6-4	2nd	▼	1.5	Dunn's first-inning, three-run homer sets the tone.
5/21	@ Chicago White Sox	L	3-1	2nd	▼	1.5	Quintana shuts Sox out for 6⅓.
5/22	@ Chicago White Sox	W	6-2	2nd	▼	.5	Sox capitalize vs. Chicago bullpen to salvage series finale.
5/23	Cleveland	L	12-3	2nd	▼	1	Reynolds, Stubbs each collect three RBIs on three hits.
5/24	Cleveland	W	8-1	2nd	▼	1	Carp's three-run homer proves to be plenty.
5/25	Cleveland	W	7-4	2nd	▼	1	Lester (4 ER, 10 H) fights through seven innings on 124 pitches.
5/26	Cleveland	W	6-5	T-1st	—		Four-run ninth capped by Ellsbury double to score Gomes, Drew.
5/27	Philadelphia	W	9-3	1st	▲	1	Ellsbury collects three hits to start multi-month tear at the plate.
5/28	Philadelphia	L	3-1	1st	▲	1	Dempster solid, but Lee-Papelbon duo overpower Sox.

DATE	OPPONENT	SCORE		PLACE		THE LOWDOWN
5/29	@ Philadelphia	L	4-3	1st	▲ 1	Sox almost come back against Papelbon.
5/30	@ Philadelphia	W	9-2	1st	▲ 2	Offense abounds as Ellsbury reaches five times.
5/31	@ New York Yankees	L	4-1	1st	▲ 1	Sabathia outduels Lester.

JUNE

DATE	OPPONENT	SCORE		PLACE		THE LOWDOWN
6/1	@ New York Yankees	W	11-1	1st	▲ 2	Nava, Napoli combine for eight RBIs.
6/2	@ New York Yankees	W	3-0	1st	▲ 2.5	Buchholz throws five-inning, rain-shortened two-hitter.
6/4	Texas	W	17-5	1st	▲ 2.5	Six Sox starters collect multiple RBIs.
6/5	Texas	L	3-2	1st	▲ 1.5	Rangers reach Breslow for two runs in ⅓ of an inning.
6/6	Texas	W	6-3	1st	▲ 1.5	Ortiz's 11th homer is a walk-off to right.
6/8	Los Angeles Angels	L	9-5	1st	▲ 1.5	Mike Trout (two doubles) reaches four times.
6/8	Los Angeles Angels	W	7-2	1st	▲ 1.5	Buchholz goes 6⅔ in last start until September.
6/9	Los Angeles Angels	W	10-5	1st	▲ 1.5	Saltalamacchia homers twice to drive in four runs.
6/10	@ Tampa Bay	W	10-8	1st	▲ 2	Nava's RBI single in 14th is eventual game-winner.
6/11	@ Tampa Bay	L	8-3	1st	▲ 2	Rays score early and often against Lester (4⅔ IP, 7 ER).
6/12	@ Tampa Bay	W	2-1	1st	▲ 3	Pitching makes Nava's two-run homer the difference.
6/13	@ Baltimore	L	5-4	1st	▲ 2.5	Davis ends it in the 13th with RBI single.
6/14	@ Baltimore	L	2-0	1st	▲ 1.5	Sox get three-hit by Tillman, three relievers.
6/15	@ Baltimore	W	5-4	1st	▲ 2.5	Bailey gives up two runs but hangs on for the save.
6/16	@ Baltimore	L	6-3	1st	▲ 1.5	Davis's homer, three RBIs give O's series win.
6/18	Tampa Bay	W	5-1	1st	▲ 2.5	Four relievers each toss a shutout inning.
6/18	Tampa Bay	W	3-1	1st	▲ 2.5	Rays tie it vs. Bailey in ninth, Gomes homers in bottom half.
6/19	Tampa Bay	L	6-2	1st	▲ 1.5	Hellickson and Rays' relief corps shut down Sox.
6/20	@ Detroit	L	4-3	1st	▲ 1	Peralta homers off Bailey to end it.
6/21	@ Detroit	W	10-6	1st	▲ 2	Victorino's 4-for-5 game produces five RBIs.
6/22	@ Detroit	L	10-3	1st	▲ 2	Webster lit up as Scherzer quiets Sox bats.
6/23	@ Detroit	L	7-5	1st	▲ 2	Benoit stifles late rallies.
6/25	Colorado	W	11-4	1st	▲ 2.5	Each Sox starter records a hit.
6/26	Colorado	W	5-3	1st	▲ 3.5	Uehara records first save since being named closer.
6/27	Toronto	W	7-4	1st	▲ 3.5	Pedroia homer highlights seven-run second off Wang.
6/28	Toronto	W	7-5	1st	▲ 3.5	Uehara gets the save for third time in three games.
6/29	Toronto	L	6-2	1st	▲ 2.5	Bautista homers twice, again.
6/30	Toronto	W	5-4	1st	▲ 2.5	Pinch-runner Diaz scores game-ending run on E3.

JULY

DATE	OPPONENT	SCORE		PLACE		THE LOWDOWN
7/2	San Diego	W	4-1	1st	▲ 3.5	Lackey gives up one run in eight strong.
7/3	San Diego	W	2-1	1st	▲ 3.5	Pinch-hitter Gomes sends one over the Monster to end it.
7/4	San Diego	W	8-2	1st	▲ 4.5	Webster (6 IP, 2 ER) gets first major-league win.
7/5	@ Los Angeles Angels	W	6-2	1st	▲ 5.5	Breslow-Tazawa-Uehara combo lock it down late.
7/6	@ Los Angeles Angels	L	9-7	1st	▲ 5.0	Hamilton homers off Breslow for Angels' walk-off.
7/7	@ Los Angeles Angels	L	3-0	1st	▲ 4.5	Weaver outpitches Lackey.
7/8	@ Seattle	L	11-4	1st	▲ 3.5	Hernandez limits Sox to two runs in seven innings.
7/9	@ Seattle	W	11-8	1st	▲ 3.5	Sox win on five long balls in a battle of the bullpens.
7/10	@ Seattle	W	11-4	1st	▲ 3.5	Offense shines, and Doubront throws seven innings of one-run ball.
7/11	@ Seattle	W	8-7	1st	▲ 3.5	Nava singles to score Bradley Jr. in 10th.
7/12	@ Oakland	W	4-2	1st	▲ 4.5	Bailey, in his last game of the season, sets up for Uehara.
7/13	@ Oakland	L	3-0	1st	▲ 3.5	Griffin, Balfour strand all eight Sox baserunners.
7/14	@ Oakland	L	3-2	1st	▲ 2.5	Donaldson's single in the 11th gives A's the walk-off win.
7/19	New York Yankees	W	4-2	1st	▲ 2.5	Doubront outpitches Pettitte in lefty duel.
7/20	New York Yankees	L	5-2	1st	▲ 1.5	Sox have trouble scoring for Lackey again, this time vs. Kuroda.
7/21	New York Yankees	W	8-7	1st	▲ 1.5	Napoli's HR over The Triangle in 11th gives Sox dramatic win.
7/22	Tampa Bay	L	3-0	1st	▲ .5	Moore throws two-hit complete game.
7/23	Tampa Bay	W	6-2	1st	▲ 1.5	Lester begins to return to form following 10-day All-Star layoff.
7/24	Tampa Bay	L	5-1	1st	▲ .5	Price (one run, five hits, complete game) dominates.
7/26	@ Baltimore	L	6-0	2nd	▼ .5	Sox manage just two hits in seven innings off Tillman.
7/27	@ Baltimore	W	7-3	2nd	▼ .5	Drew homers twice, drives in five runs.
7/28	@ Baltimore	W	5-0	1st	▲ .5	Lester strikes out eight as Ortiz finishes 4-for-4.
7/29	Tampa Bay	L	2-1	2nd	▼ .5	Price (one run, 7⅓ innings) dominates Sox for second straight start.

DATE	OPPONENT	SCORE		PLACE		THE LOWDOWN
7/30	Seattle	W	8-2	2nd	▼ .5	Workman, Sox win minutes before acquiring Peavy.
7/31	Seattle	W	5-4	1st	▲ .5	Drew single ends 5-hour, 15-inning marathon.

AUGUST

DATE	OPPONENT	SCORE		PLACE		THE LOWDOWN
8/1	Seattle	W	8-7	1st	▲ 1	Sox score six runs in the bottom of the ninth to stun Mariners.
8/2	Arizona	L	7-6	1st	▲ 1	Home run from Cody Ross, former Sox, in 7th is the difference.
8/3	Arizona	W	5-2	1st	▲ 1	Peavy gets win after seven innings of two-run ball in first Sox start.
8/4	Arizona	W	4-0	1st	▲ 1	Doubront, Britton, and Uehara combine for shutout.
8/5	@ Houston	L	2-0	1st	▲ .5	Lefty Oberholtzer shuts Sox down in fifth major-league start.
8/6	@ Houston	W	15-10	1st	▲ 1.5	Gomes comes off the bench to knock in four.
8/7	@ Houston	W	7-5	1st	▲ 2.5	Drew's three-run homer in the ninth lifts Sox again.
8/8	@ Kansas City	L	5-1	1st	▲ 2	Lester allows one earned run in seven innings, but Chen goes 7⅔ scoreless.
8/9	@ Kansas City	L	9-6	1st	▲ 2	Despite early lead, Peavy gets knocked around for six runs in sixth.
8/10	@ Kansas City	W	5-3	1st	▲ 3	Ellsbury (4 for 5) doubles twice and drives in two.
8/11	@ Kansas City	L	4-3	1st	▲ 3	Royals do all of their scoring early off Lackey (7 IP, 4 ER).
8/13	@ Toronto	W	4-2	1st	▲ 4	Victorino's two-run single in the 11th gives Sox another late win.
8/14	@ Toronto	L	4-3	1st	▲ 3	Lawrie reaches Workman for walk-off single.
8/15	@ Toronto	L	2-1	1st	▲ 2	Buehrle tops Peavy, his former teammate.
8/16	New York Yankees	L	10-3	1st	▲ 1	A-Rod reaches twice as Soriano drives in four.
8/17	New York Yankees	W	6-1	1st	▲ 2	Ellsbury (3 for 5) leads offense with two RBIs.
8/18	New York Yankees	L	9-6	1st	▲ 1	Dempster hits A-Rod, who responds with homer.
8/19	@ San Francisco	W	7-0	1st	▲ 1	Lester goes 8⅓ innings; Victorino, Nava 3 hits each.
8/20	@ San Francisco	L	3-2	T-1st	—	Bogaerts hitless in major-league debut.
8/21	@ San Francisco	W	12-1	1st	▲ 1	Doubront cruises as Sox crush Zito.
8/23	@ Los Angeles Dodgers	L	2-0	T-1st	—	Hanley Ramirez plates both runs, Nolasco outduels Lackey.
8/24	@ Los Angeles Dodgers	W	4-2	T-1st	—	Lester sharp again, outduels Ryu; Sox keep pace with Rays.
8/25	@ Los Angeles Dodgers	W	8-1	1st	▲ 1	Peavy pitches complete game, Sox take first for good.
8/27	Baltimore	W	13-2	1st	▲ 2.5	Victorino homers twice, drives in seven.
8/28	Baltimore	W	4-3	1st	▲ 2.5	Carp pinch-hit single in eighth wins it.
8/29	Baltimore	L	3-2	1st	▲ 2.5	Tillman outpitches Lester; Machado two hits, two RBIs.
8/30	Chicago White Sox	W	4-3	1st	▲ 3.5	Uehara strikes out two in four-out save.
8/31	Chicago White Sox	W	7-2	1st	▲ 4.5	Peavy tops former team; Ellsbury three hits, two runs.
9/1	Chicago White Sox	W	7-6	1st	▲ 5.5	Five relievers throw 5⅓ innings to preserve lead.

SEPTEMBER

DATE	OPPONENT	SCORE		PLACE		THE LOWDOWN
9/2	Detroit	L	3-0	1st	▲ 5.5	Fister stifles Sox for seven innings.
9/3	Detroit	W	2-1	1st	▲ 5.5	Middlebrooks's two-run single hands Scherzer 2nd loss (19-2).
9/4	Detroit	W	20-4	1st	▲ 5.5	Sox total 19 hits, eight over the fence, two by Ortiz.
9/5	@ New York Yankees	W	9-8	1st	▲ 6.5	Victorino's 10th-inning RBI single wins it.
9/6	@ New York Yankees	W	12-8	1st	▲ 7.5	Sox reach New York bullpen for nine runs in three innings.
9/7	@ New York Yankees	W	13-9	1st	▲ 8.5	Bogaerts launches first home run.
9/8	@ New York Yankees	L	4-3	1st	▲ 7.5	Ichiro scores on walk-off wild pitch.
9/10	@ Tampa Bay	W	2-0	1st	▲ 8.5	Buchholz tosses five scoreless after three-month layoff.
9/11	@ Tampa Bay	W	7-3	1st	▲ 9.5	Carp's pinch-hit grand slam in 10th the difference.
9/12	@ Tampa Bay	L	4-3	1st	▲ 8.5	Myers's eighth-inning double puts Rays up for good.
9/13	New York Yankees	W	8-4	1st	▲ 8.5	Saltalamacchia hits second Sox grand slam in three days.
9/14	New York Yankees	W	5-1	1st	▲ 8.5	Lester outduels Sabathia; Napoli 2 hits, 2 walks, 2 runs.
9/15	New York Yankees	W	9-2	1st	▲ 9.5	Buchholz six two-hit innings; Nava 4 hits, largest AL East lead.
9/17	Baltimore	L	3-2	1st	▲ 9	Uehara gives up first earned run since June 30.
9/18	Baltimore	L	5-3	1st	▲ 8	Davis knocks in a pair in the 12th.
9/19	Baltimore	W	3-1	1st	▲ 9	Lackey dominates: 9 IP, 2 H, 1 ER, 8 K.
9/20	Toronto	W	6-3	1st	▲ 9	Lester, Uehara lead Sox to division-clinching win.
9/21	Toronto	L	4-2	1st	▲ 8	Jays relievers throw three hitless frames.
9/22	Toronto	W	5-2	1st	▲ 8	Bradley Jr. homers to score three.
9/24	@ Colorado	L	8-3	1st	▲ 6.5	Tulowitzki reaches Lackey for long ball.
9/25	@ Colorado	W	15-5	1st	▲ 6.5	Middlebrooks homers twice, plates seven.
9/27	@ Baltimore	W	12-3	1st	▲ 7	Ortiz (three RBIs) tallies 30th homer.
9/28	@ Baltimore	L	6-5	1st	▲ 7	Despite loss, AL's best record is solidified.
9/29	@ Baltimore	L	7-6	1st	▲ 6	Six Sox starters get two hits apiece in final tune-up.

'WE'VE BEEN VERY WELL PREPARED, AND THAT SHOWS UP IN A LOT OF WAYS.

We'll make a play because a guy is in the right spot, or make a pitch because the catcher did his homework, or steal a base because we've found a situation that works. And I'm not sure I can remember a game when we didn't play for all 27 outs. Every team kind of says that, but I think we've actually done it. I'm proud of that.'

Red Sox general manager BEN CHERINGTON

skipper john farrell

BY KEVIN PAUL DUPONT • Globe Staff

They are the John Farrell Red Sox, with their lumberjack beards, colorful tattoos, and glittering bling, none of which has anything to do with the image their square-jawed, clean-shaven manager projects. Parked next to his ragtag bunch, the 6-foot-4-inch, 51-year-old skipper at first glance appears to have walked onto the wrong set, straying from his leading man's role in some PBS documentary on the thinking man's manager into a land that time — and grooming tools — forgot.

But as Red Sox Nation learned to its delight in 2004 — when the self-anointed "Idiots" won Boston's first World Series in 86 years — looks can be both deceiving and inconsequential.

"He wants to win, that's what's important," said third baseman Will Middlebrooks. "He doesn't care if we dye our hair purple. If that's what's going to bring us together ... then that's what it's about."

Farrell, one of a New Jersey lobsterman's six children, was hired just a year ago, brought back in the choppy wake of Bobby Valentine's zany and disastrous one-year tour as Boston manager. Previously the Sox pitching coach for four years (2007-10) under manager Terry Francona, Farrell left to become the Blue Jays skipper in 2011. Out was his only way up, as no one at the time was thinking that Francona was going anywhere but directly to the Red Sox Hall of Fame.

Abruptly discharged after the club's spectacular September failings of 2011, Francona had played a lead role in coaxing Farrell to take the pitching coach job here in 2007. Farrell by that time had logged a handful of years in the Cleveland front office as director of the Indians farm system, seemingly on course one day to be a general manager.

"He is such an intelligent guy, and he is so well-rounded, that whatever path he took he was probably going to be whatever he wanted," Francona said. "We were just fortunate enough for him to be the pitching coach in Boston, or he probably would be a general manager right now."

One of Farrell's teammates during their playing days in Cleveland, where Farrell went an impressive 14-10 in his second season (1988), Francona recalled driving from Fort Myers, Fla., to Winter Haven to convince his old pal to join his staff. "We talked for hours because that is such an important choice," said Francona. "And [even] without experience, I thought he would be really good — and we were right."

Farrell grew up in Monmouth Beach on the Jersey Shore, and though drafted out of high school by Oakland, he opted to attend Oklahoma State. It was a smart call, as the Cowboys made it to four straight College World Series during his time pitching in Stillwater. The towering righthander was drafted again in 1984 and turned pro with the Cleveland organization, making his major league debut in 1987.

A career 36-46 with a 4.56 ERA, Farrell battled through a pair of elbow surgeries to keep his playing career alive, and made a comeback with the Angels in 1993 after sitting out two seasons. He went 3-12 in 17 starts, hung on for another three years, then finally called it quits in '96.

Within weeks of hanging up his glove at age 34, Farrell was back at Oklahoma State, completing a degree in business management. He also caught on as OSU's pitching coach and recruiting coordinator, remaining in that post for five years before joining the Indians' front office.

"I've always found myself in the position where I've been different from the group," Farrell told the Globe soon after he left Boston to manage the Blue Jays. "I was a person in a front office that played in the big leagues, and then I was a pitching coach that worked in a front office. I guess there's a uniqueness in the whole thing."

Consistent within all of Farrell's roles, said Ben Cherington, is what the Red Sox general manager describes as his "incredible thirst for knowledge." The lead voice in bringing Farrell back as manager, Cherington witnessed from afar Farrell's drive and persistent desire to get better when they were farm directors with opposing clubs, and then up close during Farrell's four years on Francona's staff.

"He took a different approach to the pitching job than I think most guys do," said Cherington. "He took a more comprehensive approach. He acted more like a coordinator would in football, like a defensive coordinator — he was managing a group and so he was involved in different aspects of the pitching program more than perhaps some others would.

"He is a confident guy — with his stature, he's respected," Cherington added. "But he is also a guy with a ton of humility. And the combination is very effective as a leader."

BY PETER ABRAHAM • Globe Staff

captains* big papi & pee wee

David Ortiz and Dustin Pedroia would seem to have nothing in common beyond the uniform they wear.

Ortiz is a linebacker-size slugger with a personality to match, a man unafraid to voice an opinion or live the life he has earned. If Ortiz is in the room, you know it.

Pedroia is a second baseman on the small side, a versatile player whose playful arrogance serves as a shield against those who would dare doubt him. Off the field, he is a husband and father content to lead a quiet existence.

But in the eight seasons they have been teammates on the Red Sox, Ortiz and Pedroia formed a bond that goes far beyond baseball and helped serve as a foundation for the team's success this season.

"That guy, he's like my brother," Ortiz said. "We're family."

"It's great," Pedroia said. "We've played together for a long time and we've gone through so much together, a lot of ups and downs. He knows we have each other's back."

When the Red Sox started the process of renovating a last-place team a year ago, finding players who shared the values of their unofficial cocaptains was a starting point.

Ortiz and Pedroia became the cornerstones general manager Ben Cherington and manager John Farrell built around.

"We can't overstate that influence," Farrell said. "As every new player comes here, whether it's through the system as a first-year player or a guy who has signed here in the offseason or through trade, they're going to look to David and Dustin as the guys who have the most experience here in Boston."

Whether it's understanding the expectations of a demanding fan base or dealing with the media, Ortiz and Pedroia are clubhouse resources for players of all backgrounds.

The accomplishments demand respect. Ortiz, 37, is statistically the greatest designated hitter in history. He is a nine-time All-Star with two World Series rings.

Pedroia, 30, is a former Most Valuable Player with four All-Star appearances and a long-term contract that will make him the face of the franchise for years to come.

"They carry the torch. They have set the example," Farrell said. "They don't hold back with each other, either. While they respect one another, they have fun and yet they can get a clear message across if they need to.

"It's one thing to be a talented player and a veteran. It's the willingness to speak, because then you're holding yourself to a higher level of accountability, that sets them apart."

It's not something Ortiz and Pedroia do by design. Their style of leadership is more instinctual.

"I don't think either one of us looks at it like that. My main thing is show up and work. This is our job," Pedroia said. "I try to lead by example and David does, too. Go out and play a certain way.

"David is always in the cage hitting or watching video. Guys learn and get better from watching him do that."

That, Pedroia said, is a side of Ortiz that too often goes unnoticed.

"David is intelligent. I think that's what people don't know. They just think he gets in the box and takes a big rip at it," Pedroia said. "There's a game plan about how we're going to attack pitchers and I've learned a lot of that from David as I've gotten older.

"That's why our offense has been so good for so long. It's because guys like him think out approaches and have a plan when they go up there."

There are times when good intentions go awry. In July, Ortiz used a bat to destroy a dugout telephone in Baltimore after he struck out. Pedroia was only a few feet away and had to duck away from the debris.

"He got mad at me that day. But he knows how to settle me down," Ortiz said. "He gets on me when I'm going all crazy out there. We have a really good relationship. He does his own thing and I do mine. But when things get out of control and we have to say something to each other, we do it."

Ortiz often calls Pedroia "Pee Wee," the nickname former manager Terry Francona used.

"We go back and forth," Ortiz said. "But Pee Wee, nobody brings more to the table for us than he does. When I go back to my country, I get questions about that guy every day. I tell them the truth, he's a trouper and he's a great teammate. It has been a good friendship."

*unofficial

ace jon lester

BY DAN SHAUGHNESSY • Globe Staff

Grim. Glum. Red Sox lefthander Jon Lester last year looked like a 50-year-old coal miner who was falling behind on his child-support payments. He was joyless and angry. He was Ralph Nader. He was Bill Belichick. Lester was the personification of abject unhappiness.

He looked like Nomar Garciaparra during his final days at Fenway in 2004. He looked like a guy who was "Bostoned out." Lester went 9-14 with a 4.82 ERA for the last-place Red Sox. He hated pitching for Bobby Valentine, a hideous skipper who left him on the mound to take an 11-run beating against the Blue Jays at Fenway in July. Lester looked like he'd rather be a scuba diver for Roto Rooter.

"There's a little bit of a chip there," Lester acknowledged last February, after a workout for pitchers and catchers in Fort Myers, Fla. "I want to prove that last year was a fluke and not have it happen again.

"I don't think it's a matter of talking about last year. You can just see it in some guys. We've never had a season like that. We've never got our ass kicked that bad. It's frustrating and it's humbling. Nobody wants to be that team.

"It was miserable."

Are you happy playing baseball in Boston?

"I love baseball," Lester answered. "I love Boston. People don't see me other than the fifth day and when I'm out there, but I'm not out there to kid around. I'm not out there to joke around with hitters.

"At the same time, I'm having fun. It may not look like it, but I'm having fun. I love to pitch, I love

everything that there is to pitching. I take everything I do very serious. I want my game to go the way it should be. If it doesn't, I'm going to be [upset]."

Is he Bostoned out?

"Yeah, sometimes," he said. "Sometimes I want to strangle myself. It can be intimidating, especially when you have seasons like last year. It's tough. You know [you're bad] and your teammates are trying to pick you up and everybody else knows [you're bad] and you're trying to break even on the whole deal. You try to live with it and move on.

"If you can play in Boston and survive and do good, I think you can play anywhere."

Lester has a well-earned reputation as a mound pouter. When he gets squeezed by an umpire, or just thinks he's getting squeezed, he's demonstrative. It's a terrible habit, and it's costing him with the blue brigade.

Umpires don't like getting shown up. Lester has made himself a target. It doesn't help.

"Obviously, there's a lot of things I can improve on as far as my on-field actions," he said. "I know I've had some problems with umpires, some problems with body language at times. It's something I can get better with.

"When you're out there competing, you're not really paying attention. There's sometimes when somebody points out to me, 'You look like a baby.' I would rather somebody point that out to me than pat me on the butt and make it seem like it's OK. I would rather

somebody just come up to me and say, 'This is terrible. You need to change it.'"

Lester is still only 29 years old. He has pitched a no-hitter and been a key part of two World Series titles. He has averaged more than 200 innings over the last five seasons.

"I take my job serious. Every year, my expectations are higher," he said before this season began. "I don't think anybody wants to be in the position we were in last year. We want to be on top."

To that end, Sox manager John Farrell made Lester one of his missions this spring, and the pitcher responded. In six outings, he pitched 24 innings, allowing two runs on eight hits and four walks with 20 strikeouts. His spring ERA was 0.75.

"He's made the adjustments that we've targeted," Farrell said at the time. "It's been positive, the focus and emphasis on the work that needed to be done. Jon's gotten back to a delivery similar to what he had in the past. It's what made him one of the best lefthanded pitchers in the game."

Lester says it's all mechanical.

"It's all about standing tall," he commented. "It sounds simple, but for whatever reason I morphed into it from 2011 to 2012. I was pitching like I was 5-10 instead of like I'm 6-4. You can see it. You look at it, side-by-side, even someone who doesn't know anything about baseball can see it. I couldn't dig out. I don't know how it worked out in my head, but it wasn't good. So this spring I overhauled everything and I'm back to being me."

closer koji uehara

BY PETER ABRAHAM • Globe Staff

For most of the season, he walked the streets of Boston anonymously, no autograph seekers in his wake. It was only as the postseason neared that the souvenir stands at Fenway Park sold T-shirts bearing his name and number (19).

Not even his favorite Japanese barbecue restaurant in Boston saved a table for Koji Uehara, the nearly perfect pitcher of the Red Sox and the most valuable player of this surprising season.

"I came here to play baseball and to win games," Uehara said in September, "not to be famous. That doesn't matter to me."

But accomplishments have trumped his modesty. At the age of 38, Uehara has had one of the best seasons for a reliever in baseball history. And he has now met the goal he set years ago, to pitch in the World Series.

"I don't know if we're where we are without Koji," catcher Jarrod Saltalamacchia said before the postseason began. "You need that guy at the end of the game and he stepped up."

By almost every statistical measure, Uehara was the best relief pitcher in the American League this season. In 67 appearances, the most of his career, he allowed 29 hits over 67 ⅔ innings and struck out 94 against just nine walks, two them intentional. His two pitches, a split-finger fastball that dives down as it reaches the plate and a conventional fastball that comes in at 90 miles per hour but looks faster, were almost unhittable.

"It's remarkable," Red Sox manager John Farrell said. "Regardless of the time of the game, you're in to execute one pitch and then execute the next one. He's the epitome of that. He makes you look real smart."

The Red Sox started the season planning on using Uehara in a secondary role, somebody to pitch the seventh inning. Two former All-Stars, Joel Hanrahan and Andrew Bailey, were ahead of him on the bullpen depth chart.

"He was a strike thrower and we felt we needed that in our bullpen," general manager Ben Cherington said. "We liked him a lot based on what he had done and his personality seemed like a good fit."

Uehara had pitched well in his four previous seasons in the majors. But when the righthander agreed to a one year free agent contract last December, it merited only a brief press release. Other additions to the roster seemed far more significant.

Then Hanrahan was lost to an elbow injury in May and Bailey underwent shoulder surgery in June. The job of finishing games fell to Uehara, despite concerns about his durability. He never gave it up.

"I didn't think too much about it. I just went out and pitched," he said. "Whatever inning it is, the job is the same."

During an extended interview, Uehara gave answers with the assistance of his interpreter, C.J. Matsumoto. But he nodded his head in understanding when questions were asked, and sprinkled in words of English throughout.

Uehara is eager to bridge the cultural and language barriers present for Japanese players in the majors. He trades eagerly in the bawdy humor of the clubhouse, pokes fun at others, and earlier this season took a television camera from a Japanese reporter and pretended to interview Farrell.

"He's a funny guy. He has a good personality and he's outgoing," said first baseman Mike Napoli, Uehara's teammate for part of two seasons with the Texas Rangers and now with the Red Sox. "Koji is a great teammate, one of the best I've had."

Uehara said his team spirit stems from his time at the Osaka University of Health and Sports Sciences, where he raised his hand when a coach asked for volunteers to pitch. Once he started pitching in earnest, Uehara developed his split-finger fastball. That pitch made his conventional fastball more effective.

Scouts from the Japanese Central and Pacific Leagues, and even some in the majors, took notice. The top team in Japan, the Yomiuri Giants, drafted Uehara in the first round. Over 10 seasons, mainly as a starter, he was 112-62 with a 3.01 ERA. He won two titles with the Giants and was an eight-time all-star.

He became a free agent after the 2008 season. He signed with the Baltimore Orioles and was initially a starter before a series of injuries led to his becoming a reliever. In shorter stints, Uehara excelled. But the Orioles traded him to the Rangers in 2011.

When the Red Sox offered him a one-year contract worth $4.25 million, Uehara took it. The deal included an option for 2014 based on playing time that has been met. But he cares more about his unprecedented run.

"I can't lose focus on what I'm doing," Uehara said as the postseason approached. "I think about the next pitch, the next batter. That's it."

2013 BOSTON

POSITION PLAYERS

BOGAERTS

HR 1
RBI 5
BA .250
ABs 44

Youngest Red Sox (21) to start in postseason

XANDER
72

BRADLEY JR.

HR 3
RBI 10
BA .189
ABs 95

1st-round pick (No. 40) in 2011 draft

JACKIE
25

CARP

HR 9
RBI 43
BA .296
2Bs 18

Had career highs in games (86), runs (34)

MIKE
37

DREW

HR 13
RBI 67
BA .253
2Bs 29

8 triples tied for 3rd in AL with Ellsbury

STEPHEN
7

ELLSBURY

HR 9
RBI 53
BA .298
SB 52/56

Best rate (93%) for 50-steal man since 1922

JACOBY
2

GOMES

HR 13
RBI 52
BA .247
2Bs 17

The Sox are Gomes' fifth team in six seasons

JONNY
5

LAVARNWAY

HR 1
RBI 14
BA .299
ABs 77

Had back-to-back 2 RBI games in Sept.

RYAN
20

MIDDLEBROOKS

HR 17
RBI 49
BA .227
2Bs 18

Has 32 HRs, 103 RBI in 169 games for Sox

WILL
16

NAPOLI

HR 23
RBI 92
BA .259
2Bs 38

Has at least 20 HRs in 6 straight seasons

MIKE
12

NAVA

HR 12
RBI 66
BA .303
2Bs 29

Fifth in AL in on-base percentage (.385)

DANIEL
29

ORTIZ

HR 30
RBI 103
BA .309
2Bs 38

7th 30 HR, 100-RBI year tied Ted Williams

DAVID
34

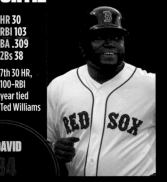

PEDROIA

HR 9
RBI 84
BA .301
2Bs 42

2nd in AL in singles, T-2 in hits, T-3 in 2Bs

DUSTIN
15

ROSS

HR 4
RBI 10
BA .216
ABs 102

Had 8 ABs with Sox in 8 games in 2008

DAVID

SALTALAMACCHIA

HR 14
RBI 65
BA .273
2Bs 40

Had career batting highs in all but HRs, 3Bs

JARROD
39

VICTORINO

HR 15
RBI 61
BA .294
SB 21/24

Tied for AL lead with 9 assists in RF

SHANE
18

EXTENDED ROSTER

PITCHER	W-L	ERA	Inn	App	GS/Svs
A. ACEVES	4-1	4.86	37.0	11	6
A. MILLER	1-2	2.64	30.2	37	0
C. MORTENSEN	1-2	5.34	30.1	24	0
A. WEBSTER	1-2	8.60	30.1	8	7
A. BAILEY	3-1	3.77	28.2	30	8*
F. MORALES	2-2	4.62	25.1	20	1

PLAYER	BA	HR	RBI	G	AB
J. IGLESIAS	.330	1	19	63	215
P. CIRIACO	.216	1	4	28	51
B. SNYDER	.180	2	7	27	50

RED SOX ROSTER

PITCHERS

BRESLOW

W-L 5-2
ERA 1.81
App 61
Inn 59.2

Has never started in 419 MLB games

CRAIG
32

BUCHHOLZ

W-L 12-1
ERA 1.74
GS 16
Inn 108.1

Has a 58-33 career record over 7 seasons

CLAY
11

DEMPSTER

W-L 8-9
ERA 4.75
GS 29
Inn 171.1

Had 85 saves for the Cubs from 2005-07

RYAN
46

DOUBRONT

W-L 11-6
ERA 4.32
GS 27
Inn 162.1

Went 3-0 in April and 4-1 in Aug.-Sept.

FELIX
22

LACKEY

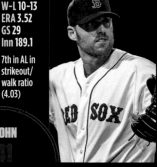

W-L 10-13
ERA 3.52
GS 29
Inn 189.1

7th in AL in strikeout/walk ratio (4.03)

JOHN
41

LESTER

W-L 15-8
ERA 3.75
GS 33
Inn 213.1

Won his 100th game in AL East clincher

JON
31

PEAVY

W-L 4-1
ERA 4.04
GS 10
Inn 64.2

Was 12-5 for Red Sox and White Sox in 2013

JAKE
44

TAZAWA

W-L 5-4
ERA 3.16
App 71
Inn 68.1

Is 8-8 in 117 games (4 starts) for the Red Sox

JUNICHI
36

UEHARA

W-L 4-1
ERA 1.09
App 73
Saves 21

Allowed just 33 hits and 9 BBs in 74.1 innings

KOJI
19

WORKMAN

W-L 6-3
ERA 4.97
AP 61
Inn 59.2

Made only 3 starts, all in April, going 1-1

BRANDON
67

> 'This group loves the attention to detail. They love to have some understanding of what they might be able to exploit inside of a game.'
>
> JOHN FARRELL

FARRELL

MANAGER
Tor., Bos.
W-L 251-235
Age 51

Went 36-46 as pitcher in 8 MLB seasons

JOHN
53

MANAGER/COACHES

COLBRUNN

HITTING COACH

Sox went from 10th (2012) to first in OBP. Hit .289 in 13 seasons with 7 teams.

GREG
28

NIEVES

PITCHING COACH

Sox went from 12th (2012) to 6th in ERA. Threw Brewers' only no-hitter in 1987.

JUAN
47

LOVULLO

BENCH COACH

Two-time manager of year in minors. Hit .244 in 303 games for 7 MLB teams.

TOREY
17

BUTTERFIELD

THIRD-BASE COACH

On Toronto's staff for 11 seasons. Has coached for Yanks, D'backs and Jays.

BRIAN
13

THE CURSE OF THE BAMBINO didn't end with the miracle comeback against the Yankees in the 2004 American League Championship Series, as cathartic as that was for Red Sox Nation. **»** "We still have another hill to climb," reminded club president Larry Lucchino. **»** Not since 1918, when the War to End All Wars still was slogging on, had Boston won the World Series, and it was fitting that the ball club standing in the way that year had caused autumnal dyspepsia for two generations of Sox fans. **»** Now, as the worst-to-first Town Team celebrates its third crown in 10 years, we're reminded that again it has come at the expense of the Cardinals, their fine-feathered foes. › PAGE 118

Cardinal outfielders confer during a Game 1 pitching change in 2013.

SOX VS C

FROM 116 • In 1946, Boston had been up, three games to two, going back to St. Louis and had ace Boo Ferris on the mound for the finale. But Johnny Pesky did or did not hold the ball while Enos Slaughter scored from first on an outfield looper, and Ted Williams, who hit .200 for the Series, sobbed in the shower.

In 1967, the Impossible Dreamers came from 3-1 down to take the Series to the limit at Fenway. "Lonborg and champagne," manager Dick Williams declared when asked about his plans for the seventh game.

But the Cardinals, irked by that prediction, bashed the weary Lonborg, who was laboring on two days' rest, and claimed the crown by a 7-2 score.

"Now it's our turn to pop off," crowed outfielder Curt Flood as he uncorked a celebratory bottle of Mumm's.

In 2004, St. Louis had the best record in baseball (105-57) and twice came back from the brink to beat Houston for the pennant. But the Sox had a whiff of destiny around them. They'd gone down, three games to none, to New York, having been booed off the Fenway diamond after a 19-8 loss, the worst in the franchise's postseason history.

But pinch runner Dave Roberts swiped second in the ninth inning of the fourth game and came around to tie the score, then David Ortiz won it in the 12th with a two-run shot into the visitors' bullpen.

The next night, Ortiz produced another walkoff triumph with a single in the 14th and Boston went to the Bronx to complete the most startling resurrection in baseball annals, winning, 4-2 and 10-3.

"How many times can you honestly say you have a chance to shock the world?" proclaimed first baseman Kevin Millar.

There was karmic satisfaction in killing off their pinstriped tormentors in the same venue where the previous season had ended in shock and "awwwww!" when Aaron "The Boonebino" Boone lofted Tim

Wakefield's extra-inning knuckler into the left-field seats. This was a different year, and the Sox had a different identity, decidedly more Stooges than Sundance.

"We are not the Cowboys any more," outfielder Johnny Damon declared. "We are just the Idiots."

If there were rules, Damon mused, his scruffy mates couldn't read them. They didn't know that they couldn't win four from the Yanks after losing three, so why couldn't they win four more? "Why Not Us?" became the mantra. The Cardinals, who'd survived their own near-death experience in the NLCS, were understandably wary.

"They showed what they can do, coming back from 0-3," observed first baseman Albert Pujols. "They never give up."

There was no precedent for what the Sox had done, so it seemed reasonable to believe that they could do even more.

"I want to see them win because it's been a long time coming," said Pesky, who'd first worn the uniform in 1942 and still had a locker in the corner by the clubhouse entrance. "I can die happy then."

The opener in the Fens began with such euphoric effervescence — a three-run homer by Ortiz and a 4-0 lead in the first inning and a 7-2 gap after the third — that fans became uncomfortable. The Series wasn't supposed to be this easy.

Indeed, four errors later — two back to-back by Manny Ramirez — it was 9-9. It took Mark Bellhorn's eighth-inning clanger off the Pesky Pole in right field to produce an 11-9 victory, the most runs by Boston in a Series game since 1903.

"That was not instructional video stuff," manager Terry Francona remarked after his fifth pitcher (Keith Foulke) was credited with the win.

The second game was, though, despite another four miscues by the home side. It was all about Curt Schilling's sangfroid and skill, spinning a 6-2 triumph on a sutured right ankle. His Bloody Sock

masterpiece in Game 6 in Yankee Stadium had saved the season, but he'd doubted that he could make it through a reprise five days later.

"I honest-to-God didn't think I was going to take the ball today," said Schilling, who couldn't walk when he awoke at 7 a.m.

It was, the righthander said, "the most unbelievable day of my life," and it sent his colleagues to the Show Me State with a mission to do what the Astros couldn't: close out the Series on the road.

Once Pedro Martinez, making his first Series start in his 13th season, was staked to a lead by Ramirez's homer and wriggled out of a bases-loaded jam in the first inning, the Sox were up and away, leading, 4-0, after five.

"One more game, one more game," Sox fans chanted behind the St. Louis dugout after the 4-1 decision.

That one game had been devilishly difficult to win for Boston.

The Red Sox had won the first two from the Mets at Shea Stadium in 1986, and were one strike away in Game 6 when Mookie Wilson's dribbler went between first baseman Bill Buckner's legs.

"Every time I see that ground ball rolling through the guy's legs, I change the channel," said Doug Mientkiewicz, who played the same position for the Sox in '04. "I don't want to see that. It plays in your mind."

As unlikely as it seemed that the Sox could blow a three-game lead, they didn't have to look back more than a week for a precedent.

"We can't take anything for granted," reliever Alan Embree said. "We proved it last series."

When the moon went into a full blood-red eclipse during the game, some Sox fans took it as a sign of the apocalypse and a Judgment Day that finally might go their way.

When Damon led off Game 4 with a homer, everything in the celestial firmament appeared aligned. As Derek Lowe, who'd won the finale of both the divisional and championship series, posted a string

1J46 | **3-2** GAME 1 | **3-0** GAME 2 | **4-0** GAME 3 | **12-3** GAME 4 | **6-3** GAME 5 | **4-1** GAME 6 | **4-3** GAME 7

Dom DiMaggio, Ted Williams, Bobby Doerr, Johnny Pesky, and Joe Dobson (top) were all members of the 1946 Red Sox who lost Games 6 and 7 in St. Louis, sealed by Enos Slaughter's game-winning dash from first base (left) on Harry Walker's double. In 1967, Red Sox rookie manager Dick Williams (above right) greeted St. Louis slugger Roger Maris before Game 2.

1967 **2-1** GAME 1 | **5-0** GAME 2 | **5-2** GAME 3 | **6-0** GAME 4 | **3-1** GAME 5 | **8-4** GAME 6 | **7-2** GAME 7

Nine days after Jim Lonborg was carried off the field on the season's final day (right), the Impossible Dream Red Sox forced Game 7 in the World Series. Reggie Smith was greeted by third-base coach Eddie Popowski after he hit one of Boston's four home runs.

FROM 118 • of zeros, 86 years of cosmic trickery appeared to be at their end.

Still, when Edgar Renteria tapped the ball weakly to Foulke and the closer prepared to underhand it to Mientkiewicz, a few middle-aged sportswriters, who'd witnessed an unthinkable moment at the same base 18 years earlier in Queens, stood and shouted, "No!" in the press box.

When Mientkiewicz gloved the ball for the final putout, the planet stood still.

"This is like an alternate reality," said owner John Henry, as the players sprayed each other with bottles of Mount Pleasant Brut Imperial. "All our fans waited their entire lives for this."

In the clubhouse, Pesky was savoring the champagne shampoo that had been deferred for 58 years.

"I knew I would see this," he said. "I didn't know if it was going to take 20 or 30 or 100 more years, but I knew I'd see it. Heck, I hope I live to see a second one."

The second one came three years later with a sweep of Colorado but it was the first one, the curse-reverser, that mattered most.

"I can't wait till next year when we go back to Yankee Stadium," said Lowe, who'd be a Dodger by then, "and don't have to hear that '1918' chant again."

As it happened, the Yankees came to them on Opening Day and applauded politely when the Sox received their diamond and ruby rings.

"It's better than my wedding ring," Damon observed. "You can always get wedding rings."

Doug Mientkiewicz (left) celebrates after gloving the final out of the 2004 World Series on a groundout by the Cardinals' Edgar Renteria. One week earlier, catcher Jason Varitek had celebrated the unprecedented comeback from a 0-3 deficit in the ALCS over the Yankees with pitcher Alan Embree.

2004

	GAME 1	GAME 2	GAME 3	GAME 4
	11-9	6-2	4-1	3-0

As strikeout victim Matt Carpenter steps away, Koji Uehara and catcher David Ross celebrate closing out the eighth world title in Red Sox history as Mike Napoli rushes to join them. Uehara allowed one run in 13⅔ postseason innings, striking out 16 and walking none. His seven saves tied the record held by four other pitchers.

2013 | **8-1** GAME 1 | **4-2** GAME 2 | **5-4** GAME 3 | **4-2** GAME 4 | **3-1** GAME 5 | **6-1** GAME 6

Mike Napoli, whose home run off Justin Verlander won Game 3 of the ALCS, celebrates his first World Series title after losing Games 6 and 7 to St. Louis in 2011. Clay Buchholz (right), who allowed one unearned run in four innings in Game 4, admires the World Series Trophy.

John Lackey, who went 1-1 with a 2.57 ERA in the World Series, tips his cap after being pulled from the game in the seventh inning. Lackey allowed one run on nine hits, striking out five and walking one.